What people are saying

Darlene Martens is a dynamic storyteller. She shares how God's amazing grace was applied to the heart-wrenching issues of her childhood. Her recurrent references to Psalm 139 reveal how God spoke the certainty of His abounding love deep into her being and help the reader take hold of this truth for themselves. Darlene Martens has come out from under the dark porch of despair into the light of God's amazing grace and abounding love!

—Sherry Stahl
International speaker, blogger
and author of *Water in the Desert*

With remarkable resilience and a captivating writing style, Darlene brings hope and healing with honesty. She unwraps this beautifully written gift through her story, layer by layer revealing God's unfailing and unconditional love. Sit back and enjoy *Amazing Grace, Abounding Love*. You won't want to put it down.

—Todd Stahl
Illustrator
and author of *40 Days In The Man Cave*

Amazing Grace, Abounding Love is a courageous portrayal of Darlene Martens's personal journey to sustain her faith in God throughout a life that has often been filled with loneliness, despair, and self-doubt. We are reminded that God is always present, especially during those moments when we are convinced He has abandoned us. This book provides us with a renewed sense of hope that He is with us always and we are all worthy of God's enduring love.

—Cynthia Kappes, MSW, RSW

[Darlene's] story touched my soul. I was reminded that I too am a child of God, I too am His great creation, and He loves me and knows my inner being. Then I cried and rejoiced for a God who not only saved me by His grace but who has shown His grace in my life, and with all of us.

—Annette

Amazing Grace, Abounding Love is a story of love and of finding the greatest love of all, again and again; the depth of Jesus's love for His daughter is astounding! One will not be able to read this story and not be changed. It overflows with the grace and truth of a girl who discovers she is never alone. Unable to put the manuscript down, I drank it in and felt the impact of her words.

—KellyAnne LaFlair
ASL/English Interpreter

Amazing Grace, Abounding Love

A Memoir of Freedom from
Depression, Lies and Abuse

Amazing Grace, Abounding Love

Darlene Martens

AMAZING GRACE, ABOUNDING LOVE
Copyright © 2018 by Darlene Martens

Some names and identifying details have been changed to protect the privacy of individuals.

This book is intended to provide helpful information on the subjects discussed, and is not a substitution for medical advice. As in all matters of health, please consult a physician before undertaking any changes to diet, exercise, and medication.

All Scripture quotations, unless otherwise indicated, are taken from the Holy Bible, New International Version®, NIV®. Copyright ©1973, 1978, 1984, 2011 by Biblica, Inc.™ Used by permission of Zondervan. All rights reserved worldwide. www.zondervan.com The "NIV" and "New International Version" are trademarks registered in the United States Patent and Trademark Office by Biblica, Inc.™ Scripture quotations marked (NLT) are taken from the Holy Bible, New Living Translation, copyright ©1996, 2004, 2015 by Tyndale House Foundation. Used by permission of Tyndale House Publishers, Inc., Carol Stream, Illinois 60188. All rights reserved. Scripture quotations marked (NKJV) taken from the New King James Version®. Copyright © 1982 by Thomas Nelson. Used by permission. All rights reserved. Scripture quotations marked (NRSV) are from the New Revised Standard Version Bible, copyright © 1989 the Division of Christian Education of the National Council of the Churches of Christ in the United States of America. Used by permission. All rights reserved.

Printed in Canada

ISBN: 978-1-4866-1703-6

Word Alive Press
119 De Baets Street, Winnipeg, MB R2J 3R9
www.wordalivepress.ca

Cataloguing in Publication may be obtained through Library and Archives Canada

This book is dedicated to:

My dear husband and best friend, Jacob, who has walked with me, shared my joys and sorrows, and loved me unconditionally.

My daughters Jaclyn, Melissa and Sheri, my sons-in-law, Ryan and Scott—as well as my grandchildren—Breanne, Tegan, Elijah, Zachary, Logan, and Adaya. Thanks for loving me and always being there for me.

My pastor and my friend, Pastor Henry and Hildi Regier, for counselling me, loving me through it all, encouraging me, and consistently pointing me towards Jesus and His love.

My brother David and my sister-in-law Doreen. They loved me as a sister and accepted me into their family as if I had always been there.

Thank you all for your love and prayers.

Contents

Preface

A few weeks following my fifteenth birthday, I was walking home from school on a cool fall day when I saw a little girl in an alley. She was approximately two years old and wore only a thin white dress. She wasn't wearing any shoes.

"Mommy! Mommy!" she cried.

As I came to her aid, the little girl's mother intervened by scooping up her daughter and reassuring her.

I don't know why the little girl was in the alley alone that day, but I do know that by the time I got home I felt quite emotional by what I had witnessed. When I told my mother, Anne, about my experience, she chastised me, saying, "You can't save them all, Darlene!"

I was shocked by her response because I had only been trying to help one little girl, one child.

Many years later, I registered for a course on family violence. The professor challenged me to deal with any outstanding traumatic issues from my childhood before completing the course; without doing so, I would be unable to effectively help others. I remembered the little girl in the alley, but I also recognized that the little girl inside me had many unresolved issues that needed to be addressed. As a result, I made an appointment to see a counsellor.

As I aimed for and received healing from the wounds that had been inflicted on me as a child, I realized that my past didn't define me—not the choices I had made, not the things done to me or said to me, and not the decisions that had been made on my behalf. I also realized that xiv • Amazing Grace, Abounding Love

although I couldn't change the past, I could change how I responded to it. I discovered that when I focussed my attention on solutions rather than on my troubles, I became more hopeful and empowered to keep going, keep doing, and keep being. But most importantly, I realized that when I turned my attention to the One who heals, then and only then could I live a fulfilled life.

I had memories stored in the crevices of my mind, some deeply imbedded and some crisp and clear as if they happened yesterday. Those memories were my experiences and I understood them from my perspective. As a result, this book has been based on a true story which has been pieced together from those experiences, from conversations I've had with people, from newspaper articles, poetry, and stories that have been shared with me. Although I don't recall the exact words used in conversations, the gist of those conversations hasn't changed the meaning of what I've tried to express. Although many individuals have been part of my experiences, other than those mentioned in this book's dedication, all names used in this book are fictional.

My hope is that you will be moved by how the Lord intervened in my life and that you will grow to love Him, the main character of this story. My hope is that you will realize how very much He loves you too!

May you recognize Him as the true Author of this story, His story. God bless!

One

Psalm 139

You have searched me, Lord, and you know me. You know when I sit and when I rise; you perceive my thoughts from afar. You discern my going out and my lying down; you are familiar with all my ways. Before a word is on my tongue you, Lord, know it completely. You hem me in behind and before, and you lay your hand upon me. Such knowledge is too wonderful for me, too lofty for me to attain.

Where can I go from your Spirit? Where can I flee from your presence? If I go up to the heavens, you are there; if I make my bed in the depths, you are there. If I rise on the wings of the dawn, if I settle on the far side of the sea, even there your hand will guide me, your right hand will hold me fast. If I say, "Surely the darkness will hide me and the light become night around me," even the darkness will not be dark to you; the night will shine like the day, for darkness is as light to you.

For you created my inmost being; you knit me together in my mother's womb. I praise you because I am fearfully and wonderfully made; your works are wonderful, I know that full well. My frame was not hidden from you when I was made in the secret place, when I was woven together in the depths of the earth. Your eyes saw my unformed body; all the days ordained for me were written in your book before one of them came to be. How precious to me are your thoughts, God! How vast is the sum of them! Were I to count them, they would outnumber the grains of sand—when I awake, I am still with you.

If only you, God, would slay the wicked! Away from me, you who are bloodthirsty! They speak of you with evil intent; your adversaries misuse your name. Do I not hate those who hate you, Lord, and abhor those who are in rebellion against you? I have nothing but hatred for them; I count them my enemies. Search me, God, and know my heart; test me and know my anxious thoughts. See if there is any offensive way in me, and lead me in the way everlasting.

You have searched me, Lord, and you know me. You know when I sit and when I rise; you perceive my thoughts from afar. You discern my going out and my lying down; you are familiar with all my ways. Before a word is on my tongue you, Lord, know it completely.

—Psalm 139:1–4

two

In the Darkness

May 1962

I SAT WITH MY BACK FLAT AGAINST THE BLOCK WALL, MY ARMS CURLED around my knees, which were drawn tightly toward my chest while providing a resting place for my chin. Tears streamed down my face as I wept uncontrollably. I was alone. In an effort to comfort myself, I rocked back and forth while my broken heart repeatedly chanted, "Nobody loves me. Everybody hates me."

I had easily tucked my small, six-year-old frame into the darkened space under the porch stairs, reassuring myself that I was out of sight. I remained quiet and hidden, my knees muffling my sobs. No one was to find me.

But after a while it became apparent that I didn't need to fear my hiding spot being found. The truth of the matter was that no one had come looking for me, at least not on this day.

When my tears finally stopped, I began to take in my surroundings. Countless bugs joined me in my obscurity, although I was certain their reasons for being there were different from my own. My goal was to lay hidden; their goal was to live out their purpose. This was their home. The centipedes, ants, and beetles actively busied themselves while enjoying the spring warmth. It was then that I realized the ground was damp and the foundation block wall behind me cold, perhaps indicative of a recent spring rain.

The longer I sequestered myself, the more comfortable I became. As my eyes adjusted to the darkness, I found it amazing that I could see through the slats of the porch to the outside world. I watched in wonder as cars sped by the front of the house. I could see them through a small knot hole, but they couldn't see me. I could see the sidewalk that led across the front of the house and recalled the fun I sometimes had when I rode my tricycle down to the neighbours' house and then home again. Then I remembered hearing my mother's warnings to stay away from the curb because of the busy traffic. Why was it that my mother didn't come looking for me now?

At that thought, I rocked myself again. "Nobody loves me. Everybody hates me."

I frequented my hideaway under the front porch many times over the next several weeks. Each time I ran there in a wave of tears, and each time I felt alone, angry, or afraid.

It was during one of these seclusions that I noticed it. There, growing in the darkness at the base of the block wall, was a wide, shiny green leaf. Over the next couple of weeks, it was soon accompanied by a few more leaves encircling a series of stems that grew up out of the centre. I wondered at this unusual sight. I had never observed a plant that closely, even those my mother grew in pots on the windowsills inside.

Over time I visited my hiding spot more as a getaway rather than a hideaway. It also gave me an opportunity to check in on the plant to which I had grown attached.

But one day, during another broken-down crying moment, my observation of the plant revealed the most beautiful upside-down white bells; they were clustered together and hung from their stems between the leaves. I noticed them when I stopped crying. Each one was so fragile, so perfectly made. I leaned over and gently placed my nose towards the tiny, delicate bells and soaked in their sweet, gentle fragrance. Somehow, even at my tender age, those flowers gave me a sense of comfort and hope.

On one occasion, my sister came looking for me. She discovered my secret spot when she slid aside one of the boards on the side of the porch; to my surprise, I saw the board move and then her head poked into my hiding place. Given that she was ten and a half years older than me, it was quite a funny sight to watch her as she got down on her hands and knees, squeezed through the opening, and crawled under the porch to join me.

"What's wrong?" Annette asked.

Her shoulder-length jet black hair was teased back from the top of her head; her bangs stopped just shy of her eyebrows and revealed her big dark brown eyes. The ends of her hair curled upwards. I had often watched her in the morning as she made great efforts to remove her curlers, flip up the ends of her hair, and then tease it incessantly to give it the height she wanted.

"Why are you crying?" she asked.

I shrugged my shoulders, not knowing how to express what I was feeling. I could only tell her what my heart understood.

"Nobody loves me. Everyone hates me," I mumbled through my tears.

On most occasions, Annette was like a mother to me. She was most often home in the evenings when our father was at work and our mother went out for drinks with her friends. It was Annette who usually helped me with my homework and tucked me into bed at night.

Annette wrapped her arms around my frail body and let me cry.

I didn't know how to tell her what I didn't understand myself. There were no words to describe to her what happened in the darkness at nighttime. I didn't know how to explain the fear that overcame me in my bed. I didn't know how to tell her that I felt unloved and that I felt in the way, especially when our mother angrily yelled comments at my father, like "She shouldn't be in our room!"

It wasn't my fault that I shared a room with my parents because our house was so small.

I didn't mind that Annette came to find me and tried to console me, but it defeated the purpose of having a hiding spot, an isolated place to be by myself. The one thing I knew for certain was that I wanted to be left alone.

Soon after that, I found a new hiding spot: the doghouse. Back in its dark corner, away from the fighting and the fear, I could think and feel. The only one who would bother me there was Lucky. But truly, he was no bother. He joined me in his house, lay down at my feet, and licked the tears off my face while I shared my woes with him. Somehow the dog seemed to understand me; he made me feel accepted and he loved me unconditionally.

It was what I needed at a time when I felt so unloved and unwanted.

three

Early Memories

BEING THE YOUNGEST OF FIVE CHILDREN MEANT I OFTEN GOT MY OWN way, and I'm certain that at times I manipulated situations in order to get it. Annette babied me, and this natural inclination of hers seemed effortless. Perhaps it was because she was nearly eleven years older than me.

But being the youngest also had its disadvantages. I was destined to never know as much as my older siblings, to never be good enough, smart enough, or fast enough. Whether they intended to say hurtful things to me or they were said in jest, I wore my heart on my sleeve and took things personally. Along with other family difficulties, this set up a complicated environment to live in.

My parents fought often, usually about money. I sometimes heard my father say, "There are too many mouths to feed! Children are just a curse!"

Since I was the youngest, I took that to mean that my family would have been better off without me. If I had never been born, they would have had the things they wanted and needed.

Living in crowded quarters should not have in itself posed problems, but my mother was simply unhappy with our living situation. In an effort to ease our family's financial burdens, she often offered to go out and get a job, even if it was just part-time. But my father would arrogantly say, "No woman of mine is going to work!"

Even at a young age, it was apparent to me that his pride seemed more important to him than his wife and children living a bit more comfortably.

My father's height, broad shoulders, and round belly accentuated the stern command and authority he lorded over my mother. So she didn't press the issue and always backed down. I never knew if she did so because she felt intimidated by him or because she thought he was right.

At times my father resorted to his own attempts to make ends meet. Perhaps these were efforts to get ahead, or maybe they were efforts to satisfy his urge to take risks. Either way, occasionally he gambled and lost an entire paycheque during a game of poker at work. The intense arguments that ensued were terrible and always ended with my mother in a wave of tears and us kids feeling numb. Consequently, my mother had the additional pressures of stretching a dollar. She did everything she could to feed and clothe her family of seven.

As a result of their financial situation, my mother was forced to shop at second-hand stores. I was with my mother on one particular shopping trip when she explored our local Salvation Army Thrift Store. She chose several outfits for me and my brothers to wear and placed them on the counter near the cashier. I watched intently as the elderly lady behind the counter picked up each item of clothing, made note of the price on a scrap piece of paper, and placed the item in a second pile. She then rolled the clothes up in some butcher paper and taped the ends.

My mother and I waited patiently as the lady totalled the numbers. Still sitting on her stool behind the counter, she finally peered over the top of her glasses as she looked at my mother. She then turned her head and glared at me. I was eight years old at the time and was pale, dirty, extremely thin, and a bit of a waif. Moreover, my Shirley Temple curls made me look like Orphan Annie.

After she sized me up and down, the store clerk once again looked back at my mother and said, "That'll be ten cents please."

I was young but not stupid, and even I knew that had to be a mistake!

Softly yet excitedly, my mother repeated to herself: "Ten cents?! Ten cents!"

Her hand shook as she reached into her blue patent leather clutch purse, retrieved two nickels, and handed them to the store clerk.

Later that day, still thrilled about the grace the lady in the store had shown to my mother and our family, I heard my father as he spoke crossly to someone on the phone.

"Listen, lady!" he yelled, his loud voice and inappropriate words expressing anger. "I don't even have two nickels to rub together!"

I was too young to understand that my father's statement was just an expression. But I took his comment to mean that somehow it was my fault that he didn't have the two nickels he needed. After all, my mother had just used two nickels to purchase clothes for me and my brothers.

Contrary to the fear his size may have commanded, my father was easier going than my mother and his leniency allowed me to do certain things I wasn't permitted to do when I was under her watch. She had forbidden me to climb the old oak tree, not because I was incapable of doing so but because she was afraid I would fall. Of course, my butt got whipped when I disobeyed, sometimes with a tree branch. It didn't matter whether my friends were there. If I needed to be disciplined, it happened on the spot. No one felt embarrassed by this, because similar things happened to my friends at their houses too.

Nearly every Saturday morning, my mother prepared a grocery list for my father. Our milk, eggs, and bread were delivered every other day to the house by the bread man, milk man, and egg man, but there were still many necessities required every week in order to feed a family of seven.

As my father got ready to leave, I heard my mother say, "Take Darlene with you, will you?"

Although it seemed like more of a command than a question, this weekly trek became one of my fondest childhood memories. I held my father's hand as we walked down the sidewalk together. I chattered as we walked and he listened; at least, I thought he did. Although I could neither understand nor explain what happened at night-time, this didn't seem to affect my relationship with my father. I adored him. I always felt so happy and proud to be with him. The difference between his height and huskiness compared to my petite frame somehow made me feel safe and secure.

Especially when he often carried me home as well as the groceries!

four

Suppertime Tales

Since my father worked steady afternoons and every weekend, he was rarely home when my four siblings and I returned from school. Therefore, in an effort to maintain as much order as possible, my mother had one firm rule: "Be at my supper table at five o'clock!"

Of course, once supper was finished, my mother barely tolerated five very noisy children and often left us with Annette to babysit while she went out drinking with her friend.

But there were evenings when my mother did stay home with us, and then our suppertime would drag on while she drilled us with questions; she desperately wanted us to know the information which she felt was important for life. Gruffly she asked questions like, "Who's the President of the United States?" She emphasized the word *who*. She became very frustrated if we didn't answer quickly enough, and she frequently repeated the question louder, as if this would help us to remember or know the answer. When someone got the question right, she would proceed to the next question: "Who's the Prime Minister of Canada?" Once again, she lingered on the word *who*.

At times, she honed in on the boys for answers, because the girls usually answered the questions correctly. Absolute tension ensued if they didn't know. At that, she called my brothers "stupid" or "stoop-niggles," whatever that meant! One by one, the boys stormed out of the kitchen. From their tears, it was apparent that they felt hurt and irritated.

Our mother often felt tired, and combined with life's many inequalities and the perceived curse of having dim-witted children, she was often provoked to anger. On one such evening, she threw a three-quart jug of milk, which spilled all over the floor. Since I had gotten the answers right, I felt that the entire situation was unfair; I ran out of the kitchen, sat in the living room, and then stubbornly declared that it wasn't my fault. I was therefore not going to help clean it up!

My rotten attitude sent my mother into tears.

After that, my siblings and I found ways to avoid her stern questioning. We would instead prod her into telling us stories of her childhood. She easily captivated our attention, fascinating us with stories about her good ol' days.

The third youngest of thirteen children, she had been raised in a small town in Northern Ontario. By the time she'd reached her early teens, the world was struggling with the Great Depression, so she knew what it was like to live in poverty and go without. Although her father had worked on the railroad, he'd also served as an assistant pastor at their local church. She told us that her fondest memory of her father was his preaching. She then attempted to emulate him by lowering her voice, raising her index finger, and shouting, "You must be born again!"

Unfortunately, he had died when she was only six years old, from injuries sustained at work.

When she was sixteen years of age, she heard that they were hiring nurses in Toronto. So she packed her things and took the bus southwest to Toronto. She arrived late at night in that big city, alone. Since she needed a safe place to lay her head, she went directly to the Toronto General Hospital and knocked on the door of the nurses' dormitory. While waiting for someone to answer the door, she held her head high and stood as straight and tall as she could. She then demonstrated to us how she had straightened her back in order to make her 5'1" stature convey more confidence and maturity.

She had been intimidated by the very stern, tall, and overweight woman who answered the door, obviously annoyed to have been awakened at such an hour.

"What do you want?" the older woman had asked while looking my mother up and down. My mother made her voice sound rasp and witch-like to dramatize the matronly nurse.

"I want to be a nurse!" she had confidently replied.

Caught in her recollection of these events, my mother then bragged to us, saying that she had responded with such conviction that she was certain the woman had been intrigued, possibly wondering what such a child had to offer the medical profession. Nevertheless, the woman had pushed the open door wide enough for my mother to enter.

"Come," the older woman had croaked. My mother's eyes grew wide and her forehead rose as she once again mimicked her. "Follow me."

Though a bit reluctant and somewhat frightened, my mother had followed the woman, knowing that at minimum she would have a place to lay her head in safety. She was led down a wide, darkened hallway, then into a room with four beds. Two other young women looked up at them from their slumber, otherwise unaffected by their presence.

My mother was directed to a bed where she put down her one small suitcase and removed her coat. The older woman then walked over to a cabinet and pulled out a white nursing uniform and some shoes. Laying them on the bed, she firmly told my mother to get some sleep and report to work at the nurse's station at the end of the hall by 7:00 a.m. At that, she bid her good night and walked out of the room.

As she slipped into her pyjamas and crawled into bed, my mother surmised that introductions would be made in the morning. She only hoped there would be a telephone nearby so she could call her own mother to let her know that she had arrived safely in Toronto.

It was obvious from my mother's descriptions of her experiences in Toronto that she had loved her life there. She had enjoyed the work as a nurse's aide and also made good friends and good money. For the first time in her life, she had been able to purchase beautiful clothes and visit a dentist. She would then smile at us, her one gold tooth glistening as a symbol of a time when she'd had money to invest in herself.

Shortly after moving to Toronto, her mother and stepfather, along with most of her siblings, left their small town in Northern Ontario and moved to Windsor. They encouraged her to join them there. Her younger sister, Victoria, arranged for her to have a job at the same nursing home where she was working, so my mother, much against most of her friends' advice due to the continued depressed situation in Windsor, packed up her things and took the journey four hours southwest.

five

Heartbeat

MY MOTHER'S JOB AT THE NURSING HOME GAVE HER THE OPPORTUNITY
to care for the elderly, but little did she know that one such elderly woman would eventually became her mother-in-law—my grandmother, Rose.
One day when she attended to Rose's room to take her vitals, Rose's son
Louis was at her bedside.

"You must be Rose's son," my mother, Anne, said to my father, Louis.

My father's heart melted when he saw my mother. He simply nodded to my mother's question, completely enamoured by her petite figure
and wide round hazel eyes which were deeply set in her round face. Her
beautifully shaped eyebrows and auburn hair gave her the appearance of
a china doll.

Her experience as a nurse's aide had given her the confidence to explain to him that she wanted his mother to take some deep breaths. Because she didn't speak French well enough to communicate with Louis's
mother, she needed his help to translate.

"He was so good looking!" my mother dreamily declared to us later,
her eyes dancing with delight. "Tall, dark, and handsome, with big eyes
and pitch-black hair. And I loved his broad shoulders."

In order to keep our attention, my mother acted out how she had
listened to the beat of Louis's mother's heart. Once again she lowered her
voice and then slowly and rhythmically said, "Boom. Boom. Boom. Boom."

She placed her hand across her breast, pretended to hold a stetho-
scope, and re-enacted how she had listened for a heartbeat. But this time

she made it clear that she was describing the quick flutter of her own heart when she thought of Louis: "Boom-boom-boom-boom-boom-boom."

While we all laughed, my mother continued.

"Then! Then I would hear him speaking French to his mother. 'Ma mere,' he said softly and calmly while touching his mother on the shoulder. 'Ma mere,' he said again."

She had been taken with the relationship between Louis and his mother, and also with the smoothness of his voice. She had understood for the first time why they called French one of the romance languages.

"I always remained professional, of course!" she reminded us.

The other nurses had teased her because they'd noticed that Louis usually came during my mother's shift. In turn, she had noticed that when he saw her, he always said something funny to make her laugh.

"And you know your father," she said to us. "He was also a big flirt!"

My father had a charismatic charm, and she had been captivated by him. When they were in public, everyone seemed attracted to his outgoing personality and confidence. When they were alone together, she was mesmerized by their conversations, fascinated by his ability to make her feel special and important.

Then there were the additional benefits: not only was he handsome and kind, but he seemed somewhat settled financially. Several years older than my mother, my father already had a steady job as a bus driver. He was an only child and his parents owned property.

However, my father felt conflicted. His parents had raised him in a very strict religious home. He had always been devoted to the faith, and he had made a commitment to them that he would one day take a leadership role in the church. He was aware that falling in love with someone from a different religious background affected that plan. Evidently, he eventually resolved the conflict he felt between his love for his faith and his love for my mother.

My grandmother gave her blessing and accepted my mother into her heart and family. She called her Oiselle, which in French means "little bird."

Before long, five children were living under their roof.

six

The Little Man Who Wasn't There

My father had a lot of responsibility: seven mouths that needed to be fed and bills that needed to be paid. But the greatest stressor in our home was the tension either between my father and my mother or between my mother and one of us kids.

My father covered those conflicts with laughter and humour, trying to keep the mood light. He did his best to turn angry situations into funny ones, or find funny situations to laugh about. He also enjoyed teasing us kids, and he had the ability to be spontaneously witty when unusual things happened.

This was true when, one hot summer day, a cold glass of iced tea suddenly shifted in its newfound puddle of condensation. My father acted shocked, shrugged his shoulders, and declared, "Who did that!?"

I reacted in amazement.

"It must have been the little man who wasn't there," he further exclaimed. "He wasn't there again today. Boy oh boy, I wish he'd go away!"

Of course, I quickly looked around the room to find the man who wasn't there.

At other times, when there seemed to be no explanation for something in the house that had gone missing, someone would inevitably ask, "Who did such and such?" or "Who took such and such?"

That allowed my father the perfect opportunity to use his quick wit.

"Who. Who did it." He was blaming someone named Who who really wasn't there.

This either lightened the mood and made one of us kids giggle or it invoked an eye roll or headshake.

"Oh, Dad!"

Like my mother, my father captured our attention at suppertime. But his stories centred on the Prohibition and his family's involvement in attempting to legalize the sale of liquor. His upbringing had been full of adventure, risk, and excitement as his family and friends had all done their part in smuggling liquor across the Canada/U.S. border. In addition, my grandparents had hid the illegal substance in their home: under the floorboards, in the basement, and even in the walls of the wooden fence surrounding their yard.

I sensed my father's excitement well up in him when he recalled Al Capone, the gangster from Chicago who had visited their neighbourhood. My father told us that people had lined the sidewalks on Drouillard Road and waited in silent anticipation of Capone passing by, all in an effort to pay him reverence. Once Capone started his procession down the sidewalk, each person quietly whispered his name to warn their neighbour that he was coming. This created a resounding murmur along the street as his name reverberated rhythmically: "Capone. Capone. Capone."

Since my father was a tall and stocky young man, he was hired to work as a bouncer at Thomas's Inn on the shore of the Detroit River. The inn's "gingerbread entrances, mahogany panelled walls, its fabulous 'shore dinners,' [and] the hideaway gambling and plush interior, became a favourite of Detroiters."[1] Although my father's main job was to deal with the rowdies, he also played piano and helped out if there was a police raid.

When Thomas' Inn was the target of a raid, his chore was to rush to customers' tables and dump liquor from the glasses onto the well-padded carpets.[2]

---

1 C.H. Gervais, *The Rumrunners: A Prohibition Scrapbook* (Thornhill, ON: Firefly Books, 1980), 104.

2 Ibid.

If the police came, they couldn't make any arrests as long as there wasn't any liquor in the glasses on the tables. Even though the place would smell like liquor, it was one of the few ways to avoid arrest.

My father proudly shared that at the end of his shift, his job was to tally the evening's earnings. He sat at a table and first sorted the coins: pennies, nickels, dimes, and quarters, each in their own piles. Then he counted the change. Over time, he learned how to periodically flick a dime off the table so that it slid down his leg and landed in the cuff of his pants. He figured that was his bonus for a job well done. I was amazed by this skill and was in awe of him, but my mother sat in disdain, sighing and rolling her eyes.

My father attributed his ability to play piano to the stern insistence of his music teachers at his church school. They had not only taught him how to play but also insisted that he play well. They even ensured that his hands looked good on the keys. According to my father, they insisted that his fingernails be well-groomed, and the cuticles needed to be pushed back to such a point that there was a full half-moon showing under the nailbed. If he didn't comply, his knuckles got whacked with a ruler. Furthermore, if he didn't play his scales or pieces accurately, his knuckles once again got walloped.

Playing piano became an additional skill he used while at the inn. However, he no longer played church music; nightclub songs became his new forte.

As a child, I often listened to him play our family piano. He tickled the ivories and stomped his foot with such proficiency and dexterity that the piano actually bounced in rhythm with the songs.

You hem me in behind and before, and you lay your hand upon me. Such knowledge is too wonderful for me, too lofty for me to attain. Where can I go from your Spirit? Where can I flee from your presence?
—Psalm 139:5–7

seven

Faith of a Child

1964

THE WARM SUN SHONE ON MY BACK AS I SKIPPED HOME FROM SCHOOL one beautiful spring day. When my mother saw me, she called me onto the screened-in veranda which doubled as my brother's bedroom during the summer months. As the screen door clapped shut behind me, I noticed that my mother's African violets had been moved onto the porch and been placed on the windowsill. Although my mother calmly sat on my brother's bed, her face looked serious. She placed her hands on my upper arms, held me directly in front of her, and made eye contact with me.

"I have something very important to tell you," she said. I quizzically looked back at her. "I need you to promise me that you will be a very brave little girl."

I nodded in agreement. "Uh-huh."

My mother worried about me because I didn't eat very well, and at eight years of age I was extremely frail. I saw the doctor often and she knew that I was scared of being poked with needles.

I agreed to be "a very brave little girl" because I thought she might have made another doctor's appointment for me.

"Today, Vanessa came to our house," my mother said next. "And when she left, she accidently backed her car over your new little kitty."

I was immediately sorry that I had promised to be brave. I wanted to scream and cry and be held by her as I absorbed the truth and impact of my loss. But since I had promised to be brave, I choked back the tears and did my best to stop my bottom jaw from quivering.

She handed me a box. "Your dad has put the kitty in this small box, if you and your brothers want to go and bury him."

I didn't want to open it. I chose to remember my kitty for how I had loved him: orange, soft, cute, and cuddly.

My brothers helped me choose a burial place by the fence near the centre of the yard. We picked dandelions and then created our own slow and methodical procession; it was sad but therapeutic. We covered the box with dirt and presented him with the flowers. Then we each said a heartfelt prayer for my kitty.

They were the sincere prayers of children, prayers like the ones we had learned in Sunday school.

Somewhere, somehow, in the middle of our family's folly we had a feeble focus on faith, a turning towards God that usually surfaced in times of need. We were raised with the certainty that there is a God who is in control and controls, who judges and punishes, and who sees all. We were taught that we had better be careful what we do and what we say.

Our mother sent us to Sunday school based on an invitation from the members of a neighbourhood church. We were invited to a backyard Bible club during the summer months and then invited to attend Sunday school that September. My father was indifferent to the idea, but my mother was thrilled that her children could learn about the Bible and about Jesus.

Sunday school was so much fun. I earned prizes if I memorized my Bible verse and I got a treat before I went home. I absolutely loved the singing and was intrigued by the Bible stories, especially the Old Testament stories about David and Joseph. I was particularly partial to the miracles Jesus performed, and the story of His birth gave our family Christmas celebrations new meaning. But what really affected me was learning about Jesus's love for me.

When my teacher taught our class about the love of God, I sat and listened intently. She explained that God loved us so much. In fact, He loved us in spite of the things we did wrong, such as lying and being selfish, cruel, outspoken, and even disrespectful to our parents. She explained that God went one step further and rather than punish us He had sent His only Son, Jesus, to take the punishment on our behalf. On the cross, Jesus had been crucified; He suffered, bled, and died as the ultimate sacrifice and expression of His love for us. It was beyond my comprehension that God could love us that much! Simple unconditional love: first He loved us, and then He took the punishment for us! The concept seemed almost absurd.

By pointing to her hands and feet as she talked, my Sunday school teacher demonstrated how the soldiers had nailed Jesus to the cross. She further explained that after Jesus had suffered and died, He was buried in a tomb, rose three days later, and still lives in heaven with His Father. She made it clear that if we believed that Jesus died for us, and asked Him to forgive us for the sinful things we had done, Jesus would forgive us.

In an effort to take it all in, I swallowed hard. Then my teacher added one more detail. She explained that God had promised that when we died, He would take us to live with Him in heaven, forever.

I had previously learned John 3:16, but on that day it came to life for me: "For God so loved the world that he gave his one and only Son, that whoever believes in him shall not perish but have eternal life."

I was part of an entire class of students who listened to her that day, yet I felt like I was the only one in the room. It was the strangest experience. I was totally captivated, as though God was talking directly to me. At that very moment, I knew Jesus loved me.

That night, while armed with this new belief, I prayed to Jesus and asked Him, in my own eight-year-old way, to forgive me for my sins and come into my heart. I told him that I believed He had died for *me* and that He loved *me*! I remember asking Him to wash me and make me as white as snow. I cried myself to sleep as I felt His love cover me like a warm soft blanket.

Jesus loved me.

eight

Dead Woman Under the Pussy Willow Bush

My brother Stewart and I were extremely excited when friends of my parents stopped by our house to visit. One day, these friends brought their two children for us to play with. We begged to go to the corner store that day to purchase popsicles for the four of us, and our parents reluctantly gave their permission as long as we promised to be very careful crossing the busy road to and from the store.

Stewart and I walked together down the sidewalk, carefully crossed the road, and entered the corner store. We opened the cooler and gazed in wonderment at the variety of flavours and colours. We had done the math: each popsicle had two sticks, which meant two popsicles gave us four sticks, one stick for each child. Stewart proudly paid the man behind the counter and we headed home.

Once again we safely crossed the busy road. But rather than walk around the block, Stewart wanted to take a shortcut through a field which led directly to our house. When I protested, because I had seen some dogs there earlier in the day, Stewart accused me of being a sissy.

I gave in and we went Stewart's way.

When we arrived at the centre of the field, we discovered a woman lying under a pussy willow bush. She was curled up in a foetal position with her hands folded under her head. She was shabbily dressed and using her light blue patent leather clutch purse as a pillow.

"Hey, lady!" we cried out.

But she didn't move.

"Hey lady!" we yelled at her again.

Again she didn't move. We each poked her with a stick, but she remained still.

"I know what to do!" Stewart confidently said. "I'll take her purse. That'll wake her up for sure!"

Stewart yanked her purse out from beneath her head, causing her head to hit the ground with a thud.

When the woman still didn't awaken, we were convinced she was dead. We raced towards home, certain that death itself would grab us too and plunge us under the same pussy willow bush.

"She's dead," we screamed as we ran. "She's dead!"

Since Stewart was nearly two years older than me, he ran faster and his voice carried to the house while muffling out my own cries.

Certain that I had been hit by a car, our parents and their friends came running out of the house. When my mother saw me, she grabbed me by the shoulders, shook me, and yelled at me to never play such a mean trick like that again! We breathlessly explained that it wasn't me who we were yelling about, but the "dead lady" under the pussy willow bush.

Filled with curiosity, everyone headed off to the field to assess the situation. My mother, our two friends, their parents, Stewart, and I all watched as my father checked the woman's pulse.

"She's not dead," he declared in a cold and appalling tone. "Probably drunk! Just leave her there! She'll sleep it off."

Leave her there? I thought. *To sleep on the ground all night!? Alone?*

My heart flipped. I was unable to grasp my father's heartless position and unsympathetic response to this woman who I thought was in dire need of assistance.

When I laid my head on my pillow that night, still disturbed by this poor woman sleeping on the ground outside, I said an additional "God bless" for her.

The next morning, I ran out to the field to check on the "dead" lady. She was gone.

❧

I watched as my bed was pushed down the hall to my sisters' bedroom. Everyone squealed different orders: "Watch the wall! Push harder!"

Since their bedroom was extremely small, my bed was placed in front of the closet. This meant that my sisters would have to climb over my bed to get to their clothes from then on. They told me that I was annoying and just a pest.

The only thing we had in common was that we were all girls; our age differences of eight, thirteen, and eighteen put a barrier between us. But I didn't mind. This was a good move for me.

I felt safe.

nine

Moving

1965–1966

I SAT ON THE LIVING ROOM COUCH QUIETLY PLAYING WITH MY Chatty Cathy doll. I brushed her hair and fussed with her clothes, repeatedly pulling the string at the back of her neck in an attempt to get her to say my favourite phrases: "I love you" or "Please take me with you." My hope had been to distract myself from the commotion in the kitchen where my parents were having a heated discussion. That in itself was not uncommon, but on this particular night my mother was very emotional.

"We shouldn't have to!" I heard her yell. Her voice cracked between words. "We just shouldn't!"

Apparently the landlord had decided that he wanted to move his own family into our house. By doing so, he broke a previous promise to my father that he could purchase the house when he and my mother were financially ready. The landlord gave my parents thirty days' notice to move.

"It isn't fair!" my mother insisted.

Over the next several weeks, my mother had no choice but to pack up our belongings. I overheard her crying at night-time after I had been sent to bed. Even at ten years of age, I could tell she was struggling with the move. My mother seemed so sad; I felt sad.

During our suppertime tales, my mother had shared that when she and my father had first been married, they'd lived in one of my grandparents' houses. They'd lived a comfortable life with all the necessities, including a car, clothes, and some savings in the bank.

As a child I never questioned why we lived in a small rental house. It didn't cross my mind. After all, as a child it really wasn't my concern.

But as an adult looking back over our lives, I found it interesting to note that our suppertime tales hadn't reflected the difficult times my parents struggled with during their marriage. It wasn't until many years later, following the death of my mother, that an aunt shared what seemed to be a most incredible account about my father.

I understandably felt distressed by the news regarding my father's decisions and actions and how they impacted my mother and our family. As details regarding those events were uncovered, it certainly shed some light for me on the dysfunctional environment in which I grew up.

Their problems started before I was born, shortly following the birth of my older brother. At that time, my mother was exhausted. Rather than help her with their three small children, my father chose to help himself. He found someone other than my mother to satisfy his sexual longings. That affair set the stage for many bizarre and unwelcome events.

In these pages, I have not exaggerated the truth about their troubles. Rather, I have uncovered facts and details from a variety of sources in order to corroborate the narrative as told by my aunt.

ten

Looking Back at 1952

I HAVE CONJURED UP A SCENE IN MY MIND, ENVISIONING THE EVENTS of my parents' lives as if they were played out in an old black and white movie. I picture my mother as she waited up for my father one particular night. Wearing her floor-length, long-sleeved flowered nightgown, she nursed her newborn son as she sat in a chair by the window.

It was a beautiful April evening. The night was clear and the sky full of stars. As she swaddled her child and rocked back and forth, she might have noticed the crescent moon in the black sky: it made a perfect backdrop for lullabies and nursery rhymes, silhouetting cats that played fiddles and cows that jumped over the moon. I can imagine hearing her beautiful voice as she hummed softly. While she looked out to the street, she watched, wondered, and speculated as to where he had gone. In her exhaustion, she eventually fell asleep, her baby slumbering on her breast, comforted by the soft beat of her heart.

A police car pulled up in front of their house, awakening her. In my black and white movie, I imagine her face, revealing the angst that shot through her as she wondered what might have happened. But she recovered quickly; perhaps he had been picked up for drinking too much and spent the night in jail to sober up.

Two police officers walked up the front sidewalk dressed in their uniforms, their blue shirts buttoned up to the neck and their narrow black ties matching their dress pants. Their black shoes were polished to a reflective shine.

When my mother answered the knock at the door, out of respect, the police officers removed their hats as they greeted her.

"Ma'am," one officer said politely. "Can we come in to have a word with you?"

"Certainly, officers."

She spoke softly so as not to wake the baby. Her furrowed brow expressed concern for Louis at the same time that she prepared herself for their news. With due respect, she stepped aside and invited them in.

"Ma'am," the officer continued. "Tonight your husband didn't return to the station following his final bus run."

Of course, I have no idea what that scene would have actually entailed, but given the information shared with me it makes sense that it played out this way.

The police might have then continued with something like this: "His supervisor radioed him on several occasions, but as time went by he got suspicious that something was up, so he called us. We followed the route his bus would have taken, but couldn't find him. After thoroughly searching the downtown area, this morning we found his bus parked down at Dieppe Park by the river. We found this for you on the driver's seat of the bus."

The police provided my mother with an envelope addressed to her. I wonder whether her hand shook and if her body felt numb as she reached for it. I also wonder whether she recognized my father's handwriting.

I imagine that she didn't know what to do next. Was she petrified of the envelope's contents? Knowing the rest of the story, I know that at some point the police asked her to open the envelope in hopes that it might hold some clues regarding her husband's whereabouts.

When I think about my father leaving her an envelope, I wonder how long she might have stared at it, curious about what was written inside. At the same time, I imagine that her heart and mind were full of trepidation. Had she suspected that he had left her? I wonder whether her legs were weak as she slowly opened the envelope. I asked myself, if I had been in that situation, how would I have handled what happened next?

I cannot imagine how my mother must have felt when she opened the envelope and discovered that it was not a "Dear Jane" letter, but rather a suicide note.

My father was usually a man of few words, but the newspaper reported that he left a lengthy letter rather than a brief note. I have imagined many times what the letter might have said, and I have even tried to guess whether he blamed her for wanting to take his own life. All kinds of speculations have crossed my mind. I've had a difficult time processing that unbelievable act.

I visualize her legs giving out from under her as her head began to spin. I picture the two officers as they caught her by the arm and eased her into a chair in the living room while they tried to support the baby who was still asleep on her breast.

With her permission, they read the letter and then gently and respectfully asked if there was someone she wanted them to call.

It is my understanding that her brother George was the first person to come to mind, and that he arrived as quickly as he could. He was also in a state of shock when he heard the news; apparently he had recently seen Louis and he had seemed just fine.

At that point, the police told my mother that they would start dragging the Detroit River to try to locate his body. However, given the spring thaw and the strong current they speculated that it could be weeks or even months before his body was found.

My mother's world crumbled around her. Over the next few months she fell into a depression, unable to function and care for three small children. The extended family pulled together and helped out with groceries, other household expenses, and with the care of the children. As a result, my oldest sister remained with my mother while my second oldest sister stayed with an aunt and uncle. It is unknown who cared for the baby.

After this, they waited to hear news from the police.

eleven

Incomprehensible

IN AN EFFORT TO PULL OFF HIS PLAN OF A FEIGNED SUICIDE, MY father spread his belongings along the riverfront: his hat, his keys, his nail clippers, his shoes, etc. It's not known what his real intentions were. Perhaps his plan was to trigger an insurance policy payout, or perhaps it was to bring an end to his marriage. Either way, he must have known that his actions would have intensely hurt my mother.

It's incomprehensible to me that he would have taken such a coward's way out rather than tell my mother he'd had an affair. Inasmuch as I've made every effort not to judge him or the situation, and to understand the position he was in, it still seems unconscionable to me that he would leave my mother in such a horrific way.

I was told that he ran away with someone he met while driving the bus and that he had picked her up each morning to take her to the hospital for her dayshift. She was a nurse, no less.

It isn't known how long or how often they met up. It also isn't known how long the affair lasted. But somewhere along the way, he realized that he couldn't walk away from her.

I wonder if he loved her. Or was he in love with the lies, the secrecy, the intrigue, and the suspense of it all? I presume this may have heightened his desire to cheat, intensifying his sexual desire and sexual satisfaction.

When this other woman had discovered that she was expecting and was certain that the baby was my father's, he had to do something. Clearly, from his scheming, he was afraid to tell his wife that he was going to have a child with another woman. Obviously unwilling to walk away from this new baby, he made the decision to walk away from wife and his other three children.

Thinking about the situation he was in, he must have felt stuck. But he could have chosen a better way to handle the situation.

So he developed a plan to escape—a perfect plan, simple yet detailed. This included taking the few items he needed from home. Then, on the day of his getaway, he left for work as usual, saying goodbye to Anne, their two-year-old daughter, and their newborn son. His oldest daughter, Annette, would have already been in school.

He worked the afternoon shift, which likely ended before midnight. Then, rather than return to the bus depot, he most likely turned off the interior lights of the bus, drove it through the downtown streets, and eventually turned in at Dieppe Park, where he headed down to the riverside. There he tucked the bus out of the way where it wouldn't be readily seen.

According to the newspaper, he emptied the money box on the bus. I picture him slipping the money into his satchel, and I guess that it was a significant amount. I wonder whether he had any conscience about taking money that didn't belong to him. I also wonder if he really thought through that detail. If a man were to commit suicide, he would have no reason to take the day's fare. That may have been his first mistake.

My aunts have told me that his goal was to get to Florida, and that he would have needed the money to pay for his travels and perhaps even pay for the birth of the baby.

Based only on my imagination, I have tried to picture my father going through all the details in the dark along the river. I watch as he looked out across to the Detroit skyline, then took a deep breath while double-checking to make certain he had every detail covered.

He then placed the letter he'd written to Anne on the front seat of the bus. That makes me wonder, when did he write the letter? And where did he keep it during the day so that he could easily retrieve it? Maybe he kept it in his jacket pocket. Did he pat his chest throughout the day to ensure it was still there?

In order to gain entry into the United States in 1952, a person only needed to present their birth certificate. However, since my father wouldn't have wanted to create a paper trail, he would have avoided going through customs. After all, he intended for people to believe he was dead. It would have therefore been necessary to find a way into the States without getting caught. Swimming across the river wouldn't have been an option, since he didn't know how to swim, besides which the water at that time of year was ice cold and the current would have swept him away.

In an effort to understand my father's strategy, I speculate that the most logical means of fleeing Canada would have been through the old railway tunnel. He may have used that tunnel during his Prohibition days and therefore known how to sneak through without being detected.

It had been a beautiful April evening, warmer than usual for that time of year. After parking the bus, he would have headed on foot west along the riverfront toward the train tunnel. He had no fear of being chased this time, unlike during his Prohibition days, because no one would know he was missing until daybreak when the bus was found. Nevertheless, he must have moved quickly in order to minimize his chances of getting caught.

As he walked, he would have heard the trains along the riverfront, providing a pulsing, clanging, chugging chorus in the distance. Once he arrived at the railyard, he could have easily hidden between the trains as he moved stealthily along.

I visualize him as he approached the tunnel. Not knowing where the other woman was hiding, he gave a low whistle and then listened for her reply. I picture the two of them together, lured by the excitement of the moment as they embrace and kiss. I can almost hear them as they whisper to each other with a mix of elation and fright.

My father may have cautioned her that they needed to wait until the train passed so they could follow on foot. He would have reminded her that they needed to move quickly, also assuring her that he had enough money to get them through the next few months, at least until he could find work.

I wonder if they waited in the shadows by the trees, whether he wrapped his arms around her waist. Did she have a petite figure? I also wonder whether he took her by the hand and briskly walked into the darkness of the tunnel while following the train as closely as possible. My mind conjures up a scene of them sliding out of the tunnel and into the shadows of the trees that lined the U.S. side of the river. Then, as they slowed their walk to appear casual and nonchalant, perhaps they held hands as they headed to the bus station.

I realize that my abhorrent attitude regarding my father's philandering escapade has heightened the production in my own mind. I can only suppose that the drama I've played in my head is nothing like what happened in real life.

Then again, perhaps it is.

twelve

Man Found

I ASSUME THAT MY MOTHER'S EMOTIONS RAN WILD AS SHE WAITED for confirmation from the police that my father's body had been recovered. Apparently only a few days passed between the night when the police gave her the suicide note and the day when they returned to the home. I picture her as she braced herself to receive the worst possible news.

Instead the police sensitively explained that their initial investigation gave them reason to believe my father was possibly still alive! I wonder how my mother reacted to that new information.

The officers would have then explained that they had checked my parents' banking records and discovered that all of the money in their bank accounts had been withdrawn. If he had committed suicide, he wouldn't have needed to empty his accounts or take the cash from the fare box. Because of these suspicions, the police had suspended their efforts to drag the river for his body. They had changed the focus of their investigation.

They questioned my mother about whether she and my father had been having any marital or financial difficulties. She apparently explained to the police that she had just gone through a difficult pregnancy, followed by a difficult birth. With three small children, she was exhausted.

It seems beyond my understanding that my father could stoop to a point where he not only had an affair but then pretended to commit suicide in order to evade responsibility. I struggle with the fact that he abandoned his children and left his wife in order to be with another woman. Whatever his reasons, I feel that his was the plan of a coward.

I've tried to understand my father's logic and give him the benefit of the doubt. Divorce was rare in 1952, so did he think this was the path of least resistance? After all, a widow with three small children would have had a greater opportunity to remarry than a divorced woman. Or perhaps he hoped that she would be the recipient of a life insurance policy, unaware that they weren't paid out if the deceased died by his own hand.

I still feel bewildered and confused, but I can only imagine the wave of emotions my mother must have felt. First he was dead, and then he might be alive! I wonder whether she felt like rejoicing or killing him herself?

By then, my mother had become aware of a friend of the family who had recently left her husband. The coincidence of her being missing at the same time also raised red flags in the police investigation. If it was true that my mother knew the other woman, what must have gone through her mind?

Her? she might have thought. *He left me for her?*

While she waited for news from the police, had she grieved for my father? Or had she pined for him?

Approximately four months following my father's disappearance, my mother received a telephone call from the chief of police, telling her that her husband Louis had been found, in Florida, and he was being deported back to Canada.

According to my aunt, my father and the other woman had been living in an apartment in Florida with their newborn child.

thirteen

Guilty as Charged?

THE NEWSPAPER REPORTED THAT A PROMINENT BUSINESSMAN FROM Windsor saw my father in Florida and turned him in to the authorities. I suspect that prior to fleeing Canada, he made a connection with someone he knew in Florida, someone who arranged for a job doing what he knew well: bartending and bouncing.

I always thought my father was a smart man, but he obviously wasn't smart enough. He should have thought through the fact that if he had a connection with someone from Windsor who owned property in Florida, chances were that someone else from Windsor had connections there as well. Perhaps that was his second mistake.

Once again, while reviewing my black and white movie reel, I see the look of shock on his face when he realized the jig was up; he was panic-stricken when the police entered the lounge and approached the bar. I imagine they were dressed in black suits, white shirts, thin black ties, and Stetson hats. From the way they walked, it would have been apparent to him that they were each carrying a gun. I visualize them as they slowly walked towards my father and unbuttoned their coats, their right arms gently bent at the elbow and their hands close to their hips as they each prepared to reach for their weapon at a split second's notice. At that, my father's face showed both confusion and angst, his head turning from side to side as he surmised his situation and wondered whether he should try to talk his way out of it. In my thoughts, he looks frightened as he quickly takes in his surroundings and checks to see which side of the bar might be the easiest around which to make a quick dash. He knew full well that his large size gave him the power he needed to deal with the rowdies, but he didn't necessarily have the agility to outrun the police. I imagine the terror he must have felt, running in his mind while his feet remained motionless.

I have once again speculated here, but deep down I feel that he deserved the worst, most public and humiliating arrest. So many times in his life, my father bragged about falling into an outhouse and coming out smelling like a rose. I wonder if he counted on evading arrest again.

I have no idea what governing authority in Florida would have arrested an alien in the United States in 1952, but I suppose that one of the officers must have called out his name and showed his official credentials.

The informant, John Smith, had been waiting off to the side of the bar so as not to be seen by Louis. Perhaps when the officer announced my father's name, Smith nodded, signalling towards my father in confirmation.

"You are under arrest," the officer may have said. "For illegal entry to the United States, for starters."

Handcuffed, he was led out of the bar.

According to the newspaper, he was arraigned in court on the charge of illegal entry to the United States. It is suspected that he was also charged with working without proper written permission, as well as other minor charges. He was transported to Ellis Island in New York, where he was detained until proper arrangements were made to deport him back to Canada to face additional charges.

My father arrived at Ellis Island, also known as the Island of Tears, as a prisoner, and as such he would have headed to the Baggage and Dormitory Building, "located on the North side of the island... the epicenter of detention for non-medical cases."[3] He faced the unknown, not knowing what to expect while he waited, not knowing whether there would be additional legal repercussions, and not knowing what condition my mother would be in when he arrived at home.

It might have been degrading to enter the detention centre on Ellis Island, and he may have been nauseated by the smells of dirt, must, sweat, and urine that still lingered in the air of the old and well-used building.

---

3 *Kingston Lounge*, "Ellis Island: Baggage and Dormitory Building." May 20, 2013 (http://kingstonlounge.blogspot.ca/2013/05/ellis-island-baggage-and-dormitory.html).

He might have been led in handcuffs up a flight of stairs and then down a dimly lit hall lined with wooden doors with chicken wire windows.

As a prisoner, he might have been physically directed into one of the rooms, the door locked behind him. Sparsely furnished, that room likely held two metal-frame cots with spring coil bottoms. A mattress would have been rolled up on one end of the bed; there wouldn't have been any blankets. The bottom half of the walls were tiled, the top half painted lime green. His room wouldn't have been remodelled for a number of years, with chipping paint, dirty walls, and extremely thin mattresses.[4] This wasn't the Ritz, that was for certain.

His stay on Ellis Island, for the most part, must have been mortifying. He was a deportee, and not one for medical reasons or because he came from "an 'undesirable' ethnic or religious group."[5]

Rather, he was a prisoner and would have been treated like one. I presume that his meals would have been brought to him and he wouldn't have been allowed to leave his room other than for the purpose of an occasional shower. His room likely housed a pee pot, only emptied when he was escorted out for a shower. Given the August heat, the smell of urine would have persisted.

After approximately two weeks, he was transported by car to the Canadian border where he was greeted by the chief of the Windsor Police Department and then held in custody pending his arraignment in a Canadian court. The newspaper indicated that he was charged with desertion of wife and children, but I suspect from other details that I've uncovered that he may have also been charged with theft and/or fraud.

According to my aunt, the first time my father saw my mother again was in court. She was apparently worn out and exhausted. My father may have assumed that she would testify for the Crown, letting the court know what a jerk he had been and how he had treated her so indifferently.

This entire charade of my father's definitely tainted my opinion of him and validated many of the things I already knew about him to be

---

4   Ibid.

5   Ibid.

true. But when I was told what happened next, my personal opinion of my flawed mother changed.

Although emotionally wounded and fragile, she attended court that day with a lenient heart. She offered no rationalization as to why she still loved him and there are no reasons to explain the grace she extended to him. She apparently explained to the judge that she was willing to have him come home. She presented him with a treasured gift: forgiveness.

Given what my father had done to her, I don't know where she found the strength to forgive that man. That man whom she had thought was dead, who had feigned his own suicide, who had taken off with another woman and had a child with her, who had caused my mother so much grief. That man. That man! My father.

Unfortunately, little did my mother know at the time that my father interpreted her act of forgiveness as permission to do it again.

By the time they reconciled, my parents lost everything, including their house, their car, and all of their savings. They ended up moving frequently, sometimes every four to six weeks, and they often didn't even unpack their boxes. They repeatedly moved into deplorable conditions, filthy and mice-infested. In addition, my father had difficulty finding work because his reputation preceded him. Eventually, however, he did find employment on the railway, and they were fortunate enough to rent a house directly across the road from the railyard. It took them many years before they re-established themselves, during which time they lived in a state of poverty.

The other woman also returned to Canada with her child, and it is understood by members of my family that my father paid her child support. Although strong suspicions and some details have been uncovered regarding the identity of this woman and her child, their whereabouts and the full truth remain a mystery.

My mother continued on with her marriage to my father, even though it was pathetic at times. I wonder whether she was committed to him because she felt trapped, and I wonder whether my father stayed with her because he felt obligated. Unfortunately, beer and liquor became a regular part of their lives. When I look back over my childhood, I wonder whether the alcohol was the medication my parents needed to cover the pain of their broken hearts—my mother's especially.

So my mother packed up our belongings and prepared to move us out of a house that had been her home for eight years, a home that had resonated with security and permanence. It's possible that the memories of the night my father disappeared, and the events that followed, played havoc on her mind as insecurity and uncertainty returned. As hard as she might have tried to forget, I imagine that she would have remembered it constantly; having to move so many times must have triggered it.

She cried as she packed. I didn't know why at the time. I was only ten years old.

fourteen

Houses

1966–1967

MY PARENTS RENTED AN OLD MOUSE-INFESTED BRICK HOUSE ON THE other side of the city. On the morning of our move, as my brothers and sister and I left for school, my mother reminded us, "Do not come back to this house after school. Don't forget! Walk to our new place and we will meet you there."

My mother cleaned that old house from top to bottom, working incredibly hard. I'll never forget the black and white checkered kitchen floor, the cracked tiles needing to be replaced. But somehow my mother had the wherewithal to make that floor look like new. After she washed it, she spread thick paste wax on top. Then she wrapped a rag around an old brick and poked a broomstick into the brick's centre hole. With all her strength, she pushed that brick and rag across the kitchen floor until it finally had a glazed shine.

My job had been to sweep the kitchen floor each night after supper. I performed this task cautiously, always prepared to jump up onto a kitchen chair in case a mouse decided to feast on the crumbs I had gathered. When that happened, I was sent into a screaming frenzy while others ran around the kitchen table with a broom or a pot, trying to catch the mouse.

Because we moved so far away from the railyard, my father had to purchase a vehicle to get to work. A well-used blue Volkswagen van joined our family. The front cab held three people while the back box had two unfastened wooden benches for the rest of us to sit on.

From the time of purchase the van's starter didn't turn over properly, and since my parents couldn't afford to repair it, my father found an alternative way to get the vehicle started. While he got into the driver's seat and put the van into neutral, my siblings and I opened the double doors at the back of the van, placed our hands on the back bumper, and pushed with all our might as we ran down the street. Once the vehicle started, my father yelled at us to jump in. At his command, we threw ourselves onto the floor of the van, laughing hysterically while we attempted to close the back doors and position ourselves on the unfastened benches.

"We have big news!" my mother excitedly told my brother and me one day. "Your dad and I bought a house today! We move in four weeks."

As she described our new house, her eyes practically bulged out of their sockets. Her voice had a high-pitched tone of excitement. Her hands couldn't move fast enough while explaining the layout of our new home.

On the day of that move, my father picked up me and my brothers after school in the van and drove us to our new house. Situated just six blocks from downtown Windsor, the house sat near a corner and just half a block from the railyard that ran adjacent to the Detroit River. It was the tallest house on the street, yet certainly smaller than the one we had just left. Like all the other houses in the neighbourhood, its wooden siding was blackened from the soot which emanated from the trains' exhaust. The front steps ended just a few feet from the front sidewalk, but unlike our former house, there was a driveway for our vehicle. The backyard was taken up entirely by an old barn with the same brown-blackened boards. I remembered thinking it was odd for a barn to be standing in the heart of the city.

The interior had been finished with beautiful oak trim, including a built-in china cabinet in the dining room and an oak staircase that led up to the second floor. But the kitchen was extremely small. Since the space intended for the fridge housed a toilet, the fridge stood on the back porch. Also, there was no room in the kitchen for a table, so our table was placed in the small dining room off the kitchen. We had three bedrooms and a bathroom upstairs.

In my exploration of the house, I discovered a secret wooden door at the back of my parents' closet. The door could only be opened by lifting a wooden bar and then folding the door in half like an accordion. Once the door was opened, a staircase led up to the attic. Although it was very rough-looking and soot-covered, the large picture window provided a beautiful view of the Detroit River and the Detroit skyline.

Just a one-metre sidewalk separated our new home from the house next door, which had been divided into three very small apartments. Each apartment housed some intriguing sets of individuals.

Two brothers lived in the middle apartment, which was closest to our house. One man's name was Peter, but we called him Pete. We didn't know the name of the brother who lived with him, so we simply dubbed him Re-Pete. Every night, the two of them went to the local bar, the Drake, just three blocks from our house. As if on cue, they returned home at 2:00 a.m., sauntering, singing, talking loudly, and at times fighting with each other. When we heard them, my brothers and sister and I hopped up onto our beds and either squirted them with water or spit on them while they stood on the sidewalk just below our windows.

"It's starting to rain!" one would announce to the other.

Their reaction always sent us into hysterics. We just deked out of sight and away from our windows. Even though we knew our antics were disrespectful, they provided us with many hours of summertime entertainment.

One night, Pete and Re-Pete started a fistfight on the sidewalk. My brother and I watched the fight and quietly cheered them on until we saw Pete pull out a knife and stab his brother in the stomach—at least we thought it was Pete; it may have been the other way around. We watched as the ambulance came. Then we watched as the police frisked Pete. The situation got out of control when Pete realized, during the frisking, that he was ticklish. His uncontrollable laughter changed the mood of the situation and sent the gawking neighbours into an uproar while the police tried to contain their prisoner.

Re-Pete lived and continued living with his brother. Before long, we were once again provided with middle-of-the-night entertainment.

fifteen

Aunt Victoria and Cousin David

1968

I PICTURE AUNT VICTORIA PULLING HER SON DAVID ALONG THE sidewalk. They always walked briskly.

"Hurry, David. Come along now." She could have lowered the tone of her voice and gruffly demanded, "Hurry!"

David had no idea what the hurry was. He only knew that he was walking as fast as he could and as fast as his eight-year-old legs were able to go. The rain made the walk even more difficult, and although his mother tried to hold the umbrella over both of them, at such a quick pace he was forced to nearly run beside her so as not to get wet.

His mother ranted and raved as they walked.

"We'll straighten this out, David! We'll straighten this out!"

David didn't know what "this" was, but he did know, from the tone of her voice and the pace of her step, that it was serious.

David did his best to keep up and comply with his mother's request, because he knew it would mean trouble if he didn't. He wouldn't get a "whipping," as one of the boys in his class called it when his mother got upset with him. With David's mother, it was different. For example, she certainly wasn't like his Auntie Anne, my mother. My mother was much more level-headed, not so quick to change her moods.

David shared with me that it didn't seem to matter how hard his mother tried to be attentive to him. He always felt like she was physically present but emotionally absent. In fact, most of the time David felt like he was caring for his mother instead of the other way around.

He knew that his mother loved him, but he was very aware that she lacked in the nurturing department. She often slept for hours on end and only woke long enough to ask him to bring her another dose of medication, at which time she would ask if he had eaten.

As a result, it ended up being David who took care of David. In fact, as David later told me, his earliest recollection of caring for himself was when he climbed onto the kitchen counter at the age of three in order to independently reach the oatmeal and a bowl. Since there was no milk in the fridge, he used warm water from the tap. Porridge became his daily staple.

Then there were those times when David's mother simply wasn't there. She often dropped him off at the homes of various friends and relatives, at different times of the day or night, always declaring that she would return in an hour or two. Most of the time she didn't return for several days. He didn't know where she went or who she was with. But he learned to make the best of it.

David told me on that particular rainy day that he had wondered how long his mother would leave him at his Auntie Anne's house. Although he knew he would miss her, he also looked forward to the fun he would have with me and my brothers.

When he and his mother finally arrived at my house, although Aunt Victoria knocked, she didn't wait for anyone to answer the door. She impatiently walked right in, and naturally David followed.

"Where is she?" Aunt Victoria demanded.

"Victoria, stop!" my mother said to her. It seemed apparent to me that she wasn't happy that her sister and David had barged in without permission.

"Where is she? We need to straighten this out right now!"

I followed my mother to the front door, and when Aunt Victoria saw me her voice softened and became sickeningly sweet.

"Come here, Darlene. I want to talk to you."

I hesitated, partly because I didn't know what the commotion was all about, and partly because I understandably felt confused by the tone of her voice.

"Victoria! Leave her alone." My mother stepped between my aunt and me. "I said, leave her alone!" She then turned her head toward me, stretched out her arm, and extended her index finger. "Go to the kitchen!"

Although I felt perplexed, I complied. That was when I caught sight of David still standing in the front hallway. It was obvious that, like me, David had no idea what was going on.

As our mothers continued to argue, I felt anxious. It was apparent that they were talking about me, yet I had no idea what the issue was.

Somewhere along the way, Aunt Victoria sat down at the dining room table and again attempted to engage me in conversation.

"Come here, honey," she said again in her overly sweet tone. "I just want to talk to you."

I stayed in the kitchen, busying myself with getting dishes and silverware so I could set the table for supper.

"What in the world is going on?" I quietly asked my mother. "First she barges in here and then she demands to talk to me. I don't really want to talk to her! She creeps me out!"

"Enough, Victoria!" my mother said to her sister. "Leave her alone!"

My aunt became angry. "It's time she knew!"

"Leave Darlene alone! She's not to know. Never." My mother turned to me while I was setting the table and again directed me back to the kitchen. "Go!"

At that I wondered to myself, *Know what? What is it that I'm not supposed to know?*

I thought their conversation was very strange.

I stood in the kitchen by the stove and made funny faces and weird movements as a means of entertaining my little cousin, in an attempt to lighten the mood. But before long my antics turned to mocking and mimicking David's mother. With my shoulders slouched, I protruded my stomach while mouthing the words "I want to talk to you!"

Then, without hesitation, I re-entered the dining room, in that same mocking stance. I'm certain I knew better than to be disrespectful, but my mother neither chastised me nor corrected me. Aunt Victoria remained seated at the dining room table while David giggled.

Suddenly, everyone grew quiet. My mother busied herself with supper while I continued to go back and forth from the kitchen to the dining room while I set the dishes on the table.

It was then that I noticed my aunt's unkempt appearance: her hair wasn't brushed and her eyes were glazed over. Her poor posture seemed to accentuate her protruding abdomen and slumped, rounded shoulders. I looked at her intently and wondered whether she was under the influence of something. Was she having one of her "episodes," as my mother always called them? On this particular day, I concluded that my aunt was under the influence. There was no other way to explain her slurred words and unkempt appearance. I had witnessed other family members drinking, even the neighbours, so it was easy for me to draw that conclusion.

When Aunt Victoria stared at me, I stared back. It felt like a stand-off. After a while, however, it felt more like she was looking right through me rather than looking at me. I wondered what she was thinking. After all, I had already developed an opinion of her, based on my thirteen-year-old experience and level of maturity.

As I looked at her, I realized how much Aunt Victoria and my mother looked alike. They both had fair, unblemished complexions as well as the same round face and round body, although Aunt Victoria was certainly much heavier than my mother. The pink blouse my aunt wore that day reflected some of its hue onto her lily white skin. On closer examination, I noticed that the buttons on her blouse were boxed, and one collar was turned up, indicative of someone who had gotten dressed in a hurry. Her expression appeared sad. The argument between my aunt and my mother, whatever it was about, had upset her. I also wondered whether other stressors and difficulties had taken their toll on her and were beginning to show.

Eventually I broke eye contact as she sat still and silent for several minutes. She didn't say anything. It was as if she had given up the fight and shifted into a different realm.

Aunt Victoria looked cautiously around the room, as though concerned that someone else might be listening. Her eyes seemed to be absorbed with fear.

When she finally spoke again, her words were somewhat garbled and ran together. Her words evidenced a woman who, rather than being under the influence of something, might have been in some psychological distress. I had heard stories in the family, and I'd heard my mother on the phone many times talking to her other siblings about Victoria and her strange goings-on.

"I heard them, you know," she finally said, leaning towards me and speaking slowly and softly. She nodded her head. "I heard them talking on the other side of the wall."

After looking around again to be certain that "they" were not present, she leaned in closer, possibly in an attempt to get my full attention.

Her eyes shone with terror. "They want to kill me!"

It looked like fear itself rose up inside her. Her blue eyes widened, then retreated slightly. Her hands shook as they cradled her cheeks. Her sad and shallow smile was replaced with angst.

Her body trembled as she took in the significance of her statement. Without warning, she became very still. She stared as though looking past me. At that moment, although she was physically sitting at our dining room table, she seemed emotionally disconnected.

Fortunately, David hadn't heard what she'd said. But from the expression on my face, I worried that he would see the fear on mine.

As I retreated very quickly into the kitchen, I surmised that he had been through this before. He was much more grown-up than most eight-year-olds and had an inner maturity and self-vigilance beyond his years. I was glad he wasn't alone with her right now.

David's big brown eyes twinkled with presumably devilish delight. Perhaps he was already scheming how he would win our next game of Monopoly. His dimples were like deep crevices, showing up only when he smiled, epitomizing his joy at our planned afternoon of fun together. From past experience, we knew that our game could last several days. We would lay it out on the sunroom carpet, away from the traffic of the rest of the household.

Oblivious to any additional conversation in the dining room, the two of us turned our attention to the game, breaking only long enough to go to the table that evening for supper.

It was easy for me to play with David because he was smart enough to keep up with me. He was ahead of himself at school and had the ability to read well and count money, which provided challenging competition.

We played until bedtime, at which time it was determined that David and his mother would spend the night rather than head home. I tucked him into the make-do bed on the floor of my brothers' bedroom while his mother slept on the couch in the living room.

The house grew quiet.

sixteen

Not So Sweet Dreams

THE SOUNDS OF THE CITY BECAME A CALMING BACKGROUND NOISE. Traffic, distant sirens, and the pulsing of trains in the railyard across the road rhythmically lulled me to sleep. I shut off the worries of the day and the anxiety I felt about my aunt sleeping downstairs while I wished things could be different for David.

The house grew quiet until a sudden and stern knock on the front door stirred everyone back to wakefulness.

"Open up! It's the police!"

My father reached the door first while the rest of us stood on the stairs, peering down towards the front hallway and wondering what the commotion was all about. Unaware of what was to come, my father opened the door.

"We are looking for Victoria Meadows," the officer said.

"What's this all about, officer?"

Before the officer could respond, Aunt Victoria's voice bellowed from the living room. "That's him! That's the man who wants to kill me!"

She turned on the living room light and pointed at my father. It was obvious from his startled reaction that my father hadn't known my aunt was sleeping on the couch.

"That's him, officer!" my aunt continued. "I saw him with a hammer. He wants to kill me!"

Appalled by her accusation, my father explained that he worked afternoons on the railroad and would have arrived home from work at approximately 11:30 p.m. As was his usual custom, he entered through the basement door and proceeded up the two flights of stairs to his bedroom. However, on that particular night, as he made his way through the basement, he had picked up his hammer so he could do a chore on the second floor first thing in the morning rather than have to go back down to the basement in the morning to retrieve it. Aunt Victoria must have seen him heading up the stairs with the hammer as he passed through the hall.

"Yup!" Victoria said confidently. "I saw you for sure. Why do you think I called the police?"

My father then explained to the police that Victoria was not well. He stepped closer to the officer and quietly said, "Can we have a word on the porch?"

The two men headed out onto the porch to have a brief discussion, leaving my aunt in the living room and my mother and us children lined up along the stairs, wondering what was going on. From my viewpoint, I was certain that my father's sophisticated charm and quick thinking would influence what happened next.

Several minutes later, an ambulance pulled up in front of the house. Two men arrived at the front door carrying a gurney and were then directed to the living room. As they approached my aunt, they insisted that she go with them.

"I am not nuts!" she screamed while climbing onto the portable bed. "He was going to kill me!"

Then, with a simple "Good night" to the rest of us, the police and the ambulance left, taking my aunt with them. Nobody offered an explanation to me or to David. I held him close, reassured him, and once again tucked him into bed.

I returned to my own bed where I lay still, no longer finding comfort and peace from the sounds of the trains or the rhythm of the city. I could only hear the echo in my mind of my father's comments, my aunt's screams, and the siren of the ambulance as they took her away.

I wondered what was wrong with her.

seventeen

Lunatic Asylum

THE NEXT DAY, MY MOTHER ASKED ME IF I WANTED TO GO WITH HER to the hospital to visit Aunt Victoria.

"Sure," I responded without hesitation. "But what about David?" After all, she was his mother.

"Nope," my mother said. "Just you!"

I didn't argue. Curiosity had persuaded me and then guilt sealed the deal. I was ashamed of my mocking behaviours the day before and thought that perhaps I had been partly responsible for sending my aunt over the edge. I convinced myself that I needed to be more mature and that I should try to understand my aunt.

"What's wrong with her?" I asked.

Anytime I asked that question, my mother always gave me the same answer: "It's just her nerves."

My father dropped us off at the hospital. It was a beautiful fall day. The grass was still green and the leaves had turned colour; many of them lay wet on the ground from the previous day's rain. Fall was always a fabulous time of year for me, not too hot yet nice enough to still be outdoors.

It felt intimidating to approach the large brown brick building. By its size alone, the hospital seemed to declare itself an institution. Its small windows and few doors didn't proffer any welcome; rather, it spoke a contemptuous message: *You don't want to be here.*

"Slow down, Darlene!" my mother chastised. "I can't keep up to your long legs!"

I had already reached my adult height by the time I was thirteen and as such towered several inches over my mother.

As we walked along, I thought she appeared nervous, worried about something. She didn't smile and her eyes were a little glazed over, as though she might cry.

There on the grounds outside the building, I saw it: a sign. I don't recall the exact words on it, but I do remember that they included "Psychiatric." At that, I felt an uneasy sensation in the pit of my stomach and somehow understood my mother's nervousness. From the things I had heard in my family, I easily misinterpreted that sign to mean "nuthouse" or "crazy place for fruitcakes" or "delusional domain" or "loony bin."

My mother led the way through the doors of the hospital and signed us in. I followed closely behind, the muscles in my shoulders tightening and my upper back and neck cringing when I heard the double doors slam shut and lock behind us.

Several people dressed in white meandered the halls. At first, the only way to distinguish the staff from the patients was by their clothing: the staff wore nursing uniforms or lab coats whereas the patients wore Johnny shirts. The patients, once they were aware that we were visitors from the outside world, approached us wanting hugs and handshakes; some begged us to open the doors for them so they could escape.

Overall, it was a frightening experience.

As we walked down the hall, I felt that I had no business looking into people's rooms. But my eyes were easily captivated by patients who sat in chairs as they rocked and stared at blank walls. I heard others cry out with unintelligible words. Uneasiness stirred inside me and I tried to make light of the situation, telling myself, *This is why they call it the funny farm.* But truth be told, I wasn't laughing.

We found Aunt Victoria in her room, wearing a hospital gown similar to those we'd seen on the other patients in the hall. Much to her benefit, it seemed to hide her protruding stomach. Her hair was brushed and was slicked back off her face. She didn't wear any makeup, but her demeanour brightened when she saw us.

"You came!" she delightedly declared.

"I told you we would come today," my mother replied flatly. "How are you doing?"

Aunt Victoria motioned to me to sit beside her. But I felt apprehensive, afraid of getting too close in case she was contagious! To my delight, there wasn't enough room on the chair, so I leaned on the edge of her bed and listened while she and my mother talked.

Eventually we said our farewells and exited opposite the way we'd come, after first stopping to ask one of the nurses to unlock the door so we could leave.

Freedom.

জ

I was well into adulthood when I learned that Aunt Victoria had been diagnosed with paranoid schizophrenia.

As a child, I didn't know about that finding, so I simply accepted the opinions of my family members that she was "nutsy cookoo." Looking back on those years, there's a possibility that Victoria's siblings didn't know the truth. And if they did know, they may not have known how to support her.

eighteen

Aunt Victoria

OVER THE YEARS, MY MOTHER SHARED MANY STORIES WITH ME about Aunt Victoria. According to my mother, when she and Victoria were younger they didn't always get along because Victoria felt entitled to all of my mother's things, including her clothes and her friends. As they grew older, however, my mother admitted to herself that she really did love her sister, but she knew that Victoria still felt entitled to whatever my mother had.

Including my mother's man.

Victoria met Uncle Bill at work, and he adored her from the start. Although he was forty-five years older than Victoria, she was attracted to the possibility of a comfortable future with him because he was financially stable. My grandmother didn't approve of Victoria's relationship with Bill due to the age difference and Anne teased her incessantly, saying that Bill was just her sugar daddy. After all, he spoiled her. He did everything for her and bought her anything she wanted.

But from Victoria's perspective, as told to me by her daughter-in-law, she was apparently coerced by Bill to marry him because he had threatened to kill himself if she wouldn't. As a result, Victoria may have felt trapped.

Victoria and Bill were married when she was only eighteen years old; they had a small ceremony and a reception which included both of their families and a few of their friends. Anne was Victoria's maid of honour. Bill paid for the entire event, even arranging for flowers and photographs.

Following the wedding, Bill encouraged Victoria to stay home, take care of herself, and follow some of her interests like writing poetry and putting it to music. Before long, they were blessed with two sons: first my cousin Robert, and then his little brother, my cousin William. According to my mother, everyone in the family knew that Victoria was overwhelmed with the responsibilities of caring for a home, a husband, and two small children. My mother told me that before long Bill grew tolerant, but as time progressed he told her that he thought she was lazy; after all, it wasn't right that he had to do so much in the evening after he had worked hard all day. Victoria knew that she took advantage of Bill, but she was also aware that by the time she had changed so many diapers during the day, she was left feeling exhausted.

As time progressed, Victoria started to lose interest in the things she used to enjoy, and that included the boys and Bill. At first Bill thought Victoria was just relaxed and permissive, but in reality Victoria had become neglectful of the boys and at times didn't dress them or bathe them. In one of her poems, Victoria wrote about Robert spilling soap flakes all over the floor. She took the position that there was no need to get angry at him, because in actuality it was her fault; she should've been watching him.

Most likely, her neglect of the boys wasn't intentional. Everyone knew that she loved those little boys, but they also knew she couldn't follow through with things. Increasingly, the family became aware that even though Victoria knew that she should discipline the boys, for whatever reason she couldn't seem to do it.

From what I witnessed as a child, when Aunt Victoria came to our house, it often seemed as though her thoughts were detached from her, off in the distance somewhere. At times I had the most ridiculous conversations with her, and I can only imagine how frustrating it must have been for Uncle Bill to communicate with her. She would say things that sounded funny, at least to her. For example, she would list words that rhymed. It seemed to me that she did this just to hear them rhyme, but then she would follow it up with a giggle. I initially attributed this to her poetry writing, but after a while the nonsensicality of it all made her appear childish. At first I thought it was a game to her, but somewhere along the way I realized she really couldn't help herself.

I don't think Uncle Bill would have divorced her simply because of these behaviours. He would have done anything for her, and from my best recollection of him he was a very kind, gentle, and temperate old soul.

But according to my mother, Victoria apparently had an affair and that's what caused the breakdown of her marriage. My mother told me that my cousin David had a different father from his two older brothers, so I always assumed that the "other man," the one who broke down my aunt and uncle's marriage, was David's father. However, as I uncovered truths about my family, it came to my attention that Victoria actually had a relationship with someone else prior to meeting David's father.

Regardless who the other man was, my uncle's heart was broken. He divorced Victoria, fought for the boys, and supposedly made it known to the courts that Victoria was incapable of caring for the children. The court declared her incompetent as a mother and granted him custody.

Many years following Victoria's divorce, she met David's father, who was married to someone else at the time. Joe owned the nursing home where she worked, and Victoria believed he would eventually leave his wife and marry her. However, when she found out she was expecting his child, Joe chose to honour his marriage and deny responsibility for the child. That decision left Victoria alone and unsupported.

Victoria then packed up her belongings and moved to Montreal in the hope of giving the child up for adoption. However, when her due date grew close, she resolved to keep the baby and head back to Windsor. It's unknown if she attempted to reconnect with Joe at that point in time.

It couldn't have been easy for Victoria to raise a child on her own, given that it was the early sixties. Culturally, it was a point of shame for a woman to have a child out of wedlock, and very little financial support was available for single mothers. In addition, Victoria also struggled with the disease which left her feeling out of sorts and out of control at times.

As a result, she began drinking, perhaps initially in an effort to strangle the constant emotional turmoil. But as time progressed, the combination of alcohol and medication exacerbated her symptoms, which in turn made her feel like she needed more medication to control the illness, numb her emotional pain, and stop the delusions and hallucinations.

This destructive cycle resulted in her visiting several doctors in order to get more of the medication she needed. Over time, the abuse of prescription medication, mixed with drinking, resulted in repeated hospitalizations. It was no way to live, and it wasn't a healthy environment for a child.

Whether it was how she was wired or a consequence of her disease, Victoria was often spontaneous. Ideas would come into her mind— whether logical or illogical, it didn't matter—and she would act impulsively, behaving in rather unconventional ways.

On one occasion, when David turned six, she took him to see his father. Without telling David the purpose of their mission or the identity of the man they were going to meet, Victoria tugged David by the arm to Joe's house in order to confront Joe about David being his son. She didn't make a plan in case Joe's wife came to the door. All she knew was that she was determined to have Joe meet his son. Fortunately, Joe answered her insistent knock, appearing shocked.

"Look at him," she said when he opened the door. She then raised her voice to pierce his blank expression. "Look at him! He's your son! He looks just like you."

Joe begged her to leave his home and to leave him alone. After that, Joe apparently called her occasionally to inquire about David, but he would have nothing to do with his son.

In an effort to pull her life together, Victoria turned to her faith for support. She attended church regularly and made friends easily. Unfortunately, her mental illness—or rather, her inability to care for herself properly—prevented her from keeping her friends. She used them to watch after David while she went on drinking binges or admitted herself to the hospital to have her medications adjusted. She often thought nothing of just dropping David off at friends' houses or at our house.

Such was the case when she was admitted to the hospital that fateful night when she called the police on my father and left David with us.

nineteen

He'll Be Back!

After Aunt Victoria was admitted to the hospital, David stayed with us for a couple of months. He celebrated his ninth birthday with us and my mother surprised him with a birthday cake.

Then, on December 21, immediately following supper, a birthday cake appeared for dessert. It was my brother Stewart's birthday. He was six years older than David and built tough and strong compared with David's tall and lean frame.

Immediately after he blew out his candles, my brother turned to my father and said, "Well, let's go!"

My father stood up. "Who wants to come?"

A huge scramble ensued as everyone grabbed their coats, boots, and hats. David followed in step with the rest of us even though he didn't know where we were going.

We headed outside to our old blue Volkswagen van. My father got behind the wheel and put it in neutral while my brothers Stewart and Timothy opened the double doors at the back. Together with David and me, we pushed until we heard the engine kick in. Then each one of us jumped into the back, closed the doors behind us, and rolled around in laughter.

"Where are we going?" David asked when curiosity got the better of him.

"To get our Christmas tree!" my brother excitedly replied. "It's a family tradition. We always wait until after my birthday before we plan Christmas."

We chose the cheapest tree we could find, because my father explained that it was the most affordable. The tree stood in the corner of our living room; it was rather bare, almost needleless and sparsely decorated, but it was our Christmas tree nevertheless and contributed to a family Christmas I have remembered ever since.

"We have another tradition!" I excitedly told David, my eyes widening. "Since Stewart and I are always the first to wake up on Christmas morning, we sneak downstairs, crawl under the Christmas tree, and look up through the branches at the beautiful rainbow of lights while we wait for the others to get out of bed. Would you like to join us on Christmas morning?"

"Yeah!" That's all he could muster, but his big brown eyes and dimples expressed his excitement.

As promised, early on Christmas morning Stewart and I woke David up early. He followed us down the stairs and joined in our excursion. Before long, the others joined us in the living room. Much to my delight, and even to my secret hope and anticipation, there was a gift under the Christmas tree for David. I don't recall what it was; all that mattered was that he hadn't been forgotten.

A few days after Christmas, when I returned home from school, I ran into the house, dropped my books, removed my coat and boots, and ran upstairs to find David. But when I got to my brothers' bedroom, David's things weren't there. I headed back downstairs.

"Where's David?" I asked.

Nonchalantly, my mother replied, "He's not living here anymore. He's gone to live somewhere else."

Her response was quick and to the point. I was devastated.

Gone? I thought to myself. *Where did he go?*

I felt numb and confused as I tried to sort it out. Something didn't feel right. But since he had come and gone so many occasions, I didn't ask any more questions.

"He'll be back," I told myself. "He always comes back!"

If I go up to the heavens, you are there; if I make my bed in the depths, you are there. If I rise on the wings of the dawn, if I settle on the far side of the sea, even there your hand will guide me, your right hand will hold me fast.

—Psalm 139:8–10

twenty

Battered, Bingo, and Beer

1971

I WASN'T LISTENING TO MY HISTORY TEACHER. RATHER, I WAS captivated by the weather outside. What had started out as light flurries earlier that day had turned into a winter storm. Ice pellets were tapping on the school window, distracting me and making me wonder whether I'd have a slippery walk home.

The darkened skies on that dreary February day grew darker when I arrived home and found my mother wearing the dress which she saved for special occasions, attending a funeral or going to the hospital to visit someone who was ill.

"Your father had an accident at work," she said. "He's in the hospital with some injuries, but the doctor thinks he'll be home in a couple of days."

She hadn't asked me to be a brave little girl. Her face was serious and she looked worried.

Apparently, in order to get some shelter from the ice storm that day, my father had stood under a grain elevator which was used for emptying boxcars. The ice and snow had accumulated on top of the elevator and the built-up weight had caused the elevator to collapse onto my father. He sustained major injuries and was hospitalized for over two months.

While my father was in the hospital, my mother started drinking more than usual. Most days when I arrived home after school, she greeted me with, "Get me another beer!"

That was followed by suggestions of what I should make for supper. For the most part, I didn't argue with her because I knew she had no resolve. Rather, I prepared supper and then encouraged her to come to the dining room table to eat. Although she often made negative assertions, she and her bottle of beer joined my brothers and me at the table.

Habitually, she looked to my brother and demanded, "Take me to the bingo!"

At that, I would feel my emotions spin out of control because I would know that she hadn't been at the hospital to visit my father. I couldn't understand why she would rather go to bingo than visit him. I also knew she shouldn't go out alone, especially in an inebriated state, but I didn't necessarily want to go with her. Frankly, I was embarrassed to be with her. Nevertheless, my brother always complied with her request and drove us to bingo. While there, I did my homework while she kept busy covering numbers on her cards.

The next morning when I left for school she would sleep it off, only to start all over again.

Some days, I arrived home from school to find several men in the living room drinking with my mother. Her greeting would be like before, only now the expectation was for me to serve beer to everyone.

"Get us another beer," she would command when I walked through the door. She'd linger on the word *beer*, allowing it to echo out of the corner of her mouth. It somehow made the word sound as if it had fifteen E's instead of two.

I hadn't been sheltered from the use of alcohol, as it had always been part of our family life and certainly part of our extended family get-togethers. When one of my uncles drank, he became as gentle as a baby while another uncle got wild and mean and loud. When Aunt Victoria drank, she became bizarre and unwise. When my mother drank, she became placid and a little bit loopy.

As time progressed, I admitted to myself that my mother's drinking really bothered me, so I devised some schemes so she would drink less. At first I tried diluting her beer, but that didn't go over very well. Then I tried pouring some of her beer down the drain, but she noticed right away that there was some missing from her bottle.

Next, I came up with the idea of drinking a couple of sips out of each bottle; that way, she would have less to drink. The plan worked, and she didn't notice. Although this seemed like a logical plan, the reality is that it led to my own drinking problem. After a short period of time, I realized that I didn't like the taste of beer, so I decided to sip from a glass of wine while I made supper. Before I knew it, I was drinking at fifteen years of age.

My mother's friends would leave when supper was ready, but not until I'd gone around the room and kissed them all goodbye. The smell of their cigarette-beer breath nauseated me.

I was upset about what was happening at home, but I felt powerless to do anything about it. So I developed my own rituals to help manage the daily chaos.

First, I found ways to emotionally and mentally prepare myself before going inside the house when I came home from school. I'd stop on the sidewalk outside and anticipate different scenarios based on what condition I might find my mother in. For example, I knew that if I found her sitting on the cushion of the couch in a very relaxed manner, that meant she was sober and would greet me in a grumpy mood. This was a blessing in disguise, and it usually led to us making supper together. This also meant I could finish my homework without a lot of disruption.

However, if I found my mother sitting on the edge of the couch, I knew there would be several empty bottles of beer in front of her, and my evening would end up as previously described.

This mental preparation also helped me to focus on my homework, no matter the situation I walked into.

But one particular day when I stopped on the sidewalk in front of the house, I heard our nextdoor neighbours, Ray and Colleen, fighting. Colleen was known as the neighbourhood bootlegger. She illegally sold liquor in order to make extra money; she also sold her body for the same purpose. Colleen was often "too busy" or "too drunk" to be attentive to her children, and as a result they were severely neglected: dirty, hungry, and crying. I didn't see the children that day, and given my apprehensive mood, I could only hope Colleen wouldn't call on me to go to the store for her.

Colleen often called our house and asked for one of us to go to the corner store to buy her a tin of Irish stew so she could feed her children.

But going to the store for her first required me to go to her house to get the money, and that meant being greeted by a cocktail of bad breath, beer, and cigarettes. Then her live-in boyfriend Ray would attempt to lure me towards him by making demeaning sexual advances and comments.

My brothers and I dubbed Ray a violent drunk, as we heard him yell at Colleen at night and smack her around. To make matters worse, he had a rifle. The combination of a violent drunk and a loaded rifle occasionally posed difficulties. Once, when I was eleven years old, I heard my father shout, "Hit the decks! He's got a gun!" I dove under the bushes in the front yard and waited for my father to announce that the coast was clear. I never knew what set Ray off that day, nor did I know what calmed him down. He just returned to his house without firing a shot.

So there I stood on the front sidewalk, listening as Ray and Colleen once again battled it out. Although it wasn't necessarily uncommon to hear them fighting, it seemed to have more impact this day than normal, and I wondered whether my own future would bring about the cruel fate of drinking and violence. The thought of witnessing them fight physically sickened me.

"God!" I cried out. "If there is a God, please protect me from this kind of life. I don't want to grow up to be like this!"

This became a poignant turning point in my life, as I grew more determined to figure out where and who God was. I thought that maybe, just maybe, my life could be different.

My father arrived home from the hospital two months later. Although he was still convalescing, his return brought great joy for my mother and relief for me. Unfortunately, due to the accident, my parents fell behind on their financial responsibilities. That additional stress on their marriage resulted in both of them drinking.

One morning I found my father in our backyard, throwing up his party from the night before. When I approached him to see if he needed my assistance, he yelled at me.

As I walked away I thought to myself, *Serves you right!* I lost respect for him that day, and I later told them both exactly what I thought of them. I struggled with how I was supposed to respect them when they didn't respect themselves. I told them that I was unable to approach them with my own feelings, problems, hopes, and dreams because I always felt like I was talking to the beer rather than to them. As a result, I gave up and grew bitter. My feelings were conflicted. On the one hand, I adored my father, but on the other, I realized that I could no longer trust him to protect me.

To make matters worse, occasionally a friend of the family dropped in for a beer. But each and every time he came, he was already drunk. He would teeter in an effort to keep his balance, and he was cruel and loud. Obnoxiously loud. He was the epitome of a mean drunk, yelling at and kicking our dog. He even tried to grope and kiss my sister. My father knew that I was petrified of this man, but he would still invite him in for another beer or two.

In an effort to protect myself, I hid in the attic of our house until I knew he had left. While hiding, I would cry. I would try to find God, the one I had learned about in Sunday school when I'd been a little girl, the God whom I had invited into my heart when I was eight years old. I pleaded with God to make the man go away and asked Him to please comfort me.

The attic in that old house became my refuge. I went there often to get away and to think. When I felt alone, when I felt like no one cared, when I had no one to talk to and when I felt confused, I hid in the attic and asked God to comfort me, guide me, and hold me.

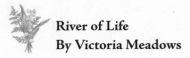

River of Life
By Victoria Meadows

When you are tired and weary
And you don't know what to say
Just put all your trust in the Saviour
Just get down on your knees, pray

And if the trials seem harder
So hard that you cannot go on
Get down on your knees and start praying
And God will send Jesus His Son

And when storms around you gather
Just trust Him a little bit more
He'll send a shower of blessings
And the rivers of life will outpour

Just when the sun starts a-shining
And you see the victory there
Don't stop your prayers but keep praying
Those prayers will help someone bear

Then you will be happy in Jesus
For Jesus your soul was won
He died on the cross of redemption
For He was God's only Son.

He is coming someday to behold
His love and it's His beauty adore
So give Him the praise and the glory
While the rivers of life outpour.

twenty-one

Too Young to Remember

It was early evening and the summer sun was still shining through the front window of the living room. We had just finished supper and my parents were relaxing and reading the newspaper. I decided that this was a good time to tell them that I felt disconnected from my cousins and that I especially missed David.

It was possible that my aggressive and demanding approach set the tone for the conversation. Most likely, my fifteen-year-old attitude of wanting things my way, when I wanted them, and how I wanted them was also a factor.

My parents immediately shifted to a defensive mode and rationalized why we didn't attend family Christmas get-togethers and why we didn't see or spend time with aunts, uncles, and cousins. Their arguments made no sense to me. They very much sounded like excuses.

But on that particular day, my mother made a comment that always stayed with me.

"You just have to understand!" she said. "It's a good thing you were too young to remember."

"Too young to remember what?" I asked.

"Anne, no," my father piped up, glaring at her. "Leave it alone, Anne." He then made the newspaper snap, adding emphasis.

My mother appeared upset. She pursed her lips and took a deep breath through her nose. "Never mind. Just never mind, Darlene."

I felt dismissed as I left the living room and made my way to the front porch of the house, where I stood and wondered, *What is it that I'm supposed to remember?*

twenty-two

Unbeknownst to me, when David left our home he was admitted to the care of the Children's Aid Society. He later told me how difficult the transition into foster care was for him, especially once he'd been moved a few times. Eventually he settled into one particular foster home where things went very well for him. His foster parents adored him and even showed an interest in adopting him.

However, due to an improvement in his mother's mental health, David was returned to her care until such time that she once again declined. Then David went back into foster care, to the same foster family that had previously considered adopting him.

At one of their first meals back together, David asked his foster father to please pass him the "mouse turds" for his hot dog. David had recalled that his foster father's reaction was quick and abrupt.

"Where did you learn to talk that way?" he demanded.

David very proudly replied, "From my Uncle Louis!"

According to David, his foster father seemed disappointed by David's change in attitude and behaviour. He told David that this type of talk wasn't appropriate. Shortly following the incident, David was removed from the home; he was devastated, as he had thought those people were going to be his forever family.

Over the next couple of years, David was moved from foster home to foster home with intermittent returns to his mother.

David's behaviour and attitude were affected by the instability in his life. He started to skip out of school and became a sassy little boy. In addition, he showed little regard for the people he stayed with. Over time, he became displeased with his mother and didn't like the way she treated him. So when he was twelve years old, he called his worker at Children's Aid and asked to be permanently removed from his mother's home. He eventually became a ward of the Crown.

Once again David was moved from one foster home to another until, at the age of fifteen, he settled in a home where he felt accepted and loved. His foster parents, Chris and Catharine, became parents to him; they protected him, supported him, encouraged him, invited him into their hearts, and involved him in their home and in their lives. As a bonus, Chris taught David about his love for stock car racing and even involved David in helping out with one of the race cars. David loved the sport and loved to race, so much so that when he was eighteen years old he raced Chris's car at Checker Flag Speedway in Windsor and won the Checker Flag!

Most importantly, Chris and Catharine loved David unconditionally.

Where can I go from your Spirit? Where can I flee from your presence? If I go up to the heavens, you are there; if I make my bed in the depths, you are there. If I rise on the wings of the dawn, if I settle on the far side of the sea, even there your hand will guide me, your right hand will hold me fast.

—Psalm 139:7–10

twenty-three

Faith Renewed

1973

BEING A MEMBER OF A WORKING POOR FAMILY MEANT THERE WAS absolutely no opportunity for post-secondary education. As such, the message in our home was clear: "When you're done high school, get a job!" It was therefore beyond my wildest imagination when a community service club gave me a bursary so I could attend college; it was enough money to pay for my tuition and books for one year. I took the bursary and registered for a Legal Secretarial course.

I loved college, made friends easily, and studied hard. Then, during my second semester, I noticed a poster in the hall announcing a Christian fellowship group. I was seventeen years old when I attended that group in the hope of finding someone who could direct me to God.

At the first meeting I attended, the youth talked about Jesus as though He were someone they personally knew. I sincerely felt in my heart that I had finally connected with people who knew God and could teach me about Him.

So, as I had done when I was eight years old, I prayed to God, asked Him to forgive me for my sins, and asked Him to be my Saviour, my God.

If we confess our sins, he is faithful and just and will forgive us our sins and purify us from all unrighteousness.

—1 John 1:9

The following Sunday morning, I went to the same church as the professor who had led the youth group at school. People there welcomed me, loved me, and taught me as I grew in my faith and knowledge of Jesus Christ.

My renewed faith in Him meant that I no longer needed to hide in attics, doghouses, closets, or under front porches, because I could hide in the shadow of His wings.

Keep me as the apple of your eye; hide me in the shadow of your wings.

—Psalm 17:8

I will say of the Lord, "He is my refuge and my fortress, my God, in whom I trust."

—Psalm 91:2

twenty-four

New Love Times Two

DAVID'S GOAL IN LIFE WAS TO WORK HARD AND BE RESPONSIBLE; HE wanted his life to be different from the life he'd had as a child. He had hoped to meet and find the love of his life, settle down, and have children of his own. That was when he met Doreen. From the start, he knew that she was the girl for him. They got along extremely well and were very compatible. He was enamoured with her beautiful blue eyes, and her lively spirit and spunk complemented his spontaneity.

While they were dating, David and Doreen talked about the importance of going to church. Even though they'd had different church traditions as children, they attended church together.

One Sunday, following a church service, Doreen and David were having a conversation when they started to talk about the Bible and what it says about salvation and repentance. Almost immediately they both found themselves down on their knees, right there in David's living room. They asked the Lord to forgive them for their sins, come into their hearts, and make them as white as snow.

That was the beginning of their walk with Jesus.

Eventually they were married. David's foster father and Doreen's sister stood up at their wedding as their best man and maid of honour. The couple felt very blessed to have them be part of their lives.

*In their hearts humans plan their course, but
the Lord establishes their steps.*

—Proverbs 16:9

twenty-five

The Right Guy

1976

I HAD PUT MY FAITH IN JESUS CHRIST; HE CHANGED ME AND HE changed my life.

I was determined that my life would change, and I set out to find a way to rise above my circumstances. I formulated a plan of action for my life and then purposed a way to put that plan into place. My strategy was simple and uncomplicated. First, I made Jesus the foundation of my life. Secondly, I wanted to make Him the foundation of my home, and in that regard I knew that I would need to marry a Christian, someone who had the same foundational spiritual beliefs I had.

I sought the Lord's direction for my life.

Whether you turn to the right or to the left, your ears will hear a voice behind you, saying, "This is the way; walk in it."
—Isaiah 30:21

I will instruct you and teach you in the way you should go; I will counsel you with my loving eye on you.
—Psalm 32:8

When I was twenty years old, I was introduced to that very special someone who not only shared my foundational beliefs, but who lived them out.

Jake was tall and strongly built, with broad shoulders. He was good looking and had dark brown hair and deep-set greenish-brown eyes. A small dimple graced his left cheek when he smiled. We met at a couple's bridal shower and only spoke for a few minutes, but then we met again at the couple's wedding where Jake stood up as the best man. He struck me as being very modest and reserved; my friend assured me that this was the case.

Given my more outgoing personality, and feeling that I had nothing to lose and everything to gain, I approached Jake after the wedding.

"Hello," I said, smiling.

His reply was simple. "Hi."

Hmmm, I thought. *A man of few words.*

I swallowed hard. "Say, I have some tickets to a lacrosse game on Saturday night. Would you like to go?"

"You like lacrosse?" he asked, seemingly surprised.

"I do. I like hockey better, but I do like lacrosse."

After a few more exchanges, and finding out the time of the game, he responded politely and matter-of-factly. "I'm sorry, I can't go. I have to milk the cows."

I thought, *Well! That's a putdown line if I've ever heard one!*

What did I know about milking cows anyway? After all, I was a city girl. So I bid him goodnight and headed home.

That week, Jake called me and asked me out on a date for Saturday night—after he finished milking the cows, of course. I was so excited. I had heard a few things about this young man: he was a Christian, he'd grown up on a dairy farm, and he was quiet and polite.

When he arrived at my parents' home, I was ready to greet him. Following introductions, we headed out to the car. As a true gentleman would, he walked around the car and opened the door for me. I turned to thank him and noticed that the zipper on his pants was down. At that, my mind went into a panic.

How do I tell him his zipper is down? I thought. *After all, I've only known him for all of five minutes.*

As we drove along, I agonized over this.

While we headed to the restaurant, our conversation was quiet and calm, mostly because I was trying to make small talk at the same time as figure out how to tell him his zipper was down. Finally, I decided that my approach would be to tell him the same way I would tell one of my brothers.

During a lull in the conversation, I rather nonchalantly said, "Jake."

"Yes?"

"I have something to tell you."

"Okay. What's that?"

My response was to the point: "Your barn door is open."

"What?" he replied without skipping a beat. "How do you know? Have you ever been to my farm?"

I was deeply embarrassed, but it was certainly an icebreaker and a chuckle that carried us through many years when we needed a good laugh.

Jake and I dated for a couple of years, and our times together were always planned around "the ladies" in the barn, as we affectionately called his cows. I don't remember when I fell in love with him, but I do know that we hadn't dated long when I realized I couldn't live without him. He was unlike anyone I had ever known: non-confrontational, a peacemaker, and patient. He not only loved me, but he was good to me. He was also faithful to God and relied on his faith to get him through his daily life. In essence, he had the qualities of a true Christian.

But the fruit of the Spirit is love, joy, peace, forbearance, kindness, goodness, faithfulness, gentleness and self-control.
—Galatians 5:22–23

Jake had been raised in a wholesome Christian home, surrounded by grandparents who lived next door and an aunt who lived with them. Sadly, his father had died suddenly of a heart attack when Jake was only ten years of age, and as a result his mother had raised Jake and his two older brothers by herself. Despite going through such a difficult time, his mother had kept her eyes on Jesus for her strength. This had impacted Jake in a tremendous way.

One evening, he told me his fondest memory of his mother. "Seeing her each morning when I would go by her bedroom," he said. "Without fail, she was on her knees by her bed, praying. Her devotion to the Lord spoke more to me about Christianity than anything she ever said to me."

Naturally, Jake's mother was concerned about our dating because our backgrounds were so different. I had grown up in the inner city and he had grown up in the country. In addition, our families and upbringings were quite opposite to each other; his parents had immigrated to Canada during the Russian Revolution while my parents had been established in Canada for hundreds of years.

However, in spite of his mother's concerns, Jake knew I was the girl for him, and he has repeatedly told me many times since, "I had no doubts that I was to marry you."

Jake loved me unconditionally and accepted me for who I was, including my quirks and wry sense of humour. His focus was not on my background; rather, it was on who he knew I was in Christ Jesus.

As we drew closer to each other, we felt it was important to also draw closer to God. So we ended each date with a prayer and committed our lives and our future to Jesus Christ, ensuring that He was the foundation of our relationship, our decisions, our future, and our home together. Jake's spiritual strength amazed me. His knowledge of the Scriptures and solid faith spoke of hope as it related to the Christian life. Jake's mother, and his brothers and their wives, also lived out their faith. They were an example to us of the importance of loving the Lord and teaching about His love to the next generation.

Although my relationship with my mother was strained, she told me that she adored Jake and was incredibly happy for me that I had found a great guy.

It was obvious that in my childhood, and even during my teen years, my father had insulted me, embarrassed me and repeatedly broken my trust. Perhaps because of his charismatic personality, I turned a blind eye to those offenses and held him in high regard. As a result, I believed that we had a good relationship. Jake, on the other hand, respected my father because he was my father, but there was an undetectable divide between them.

I was with Jake when he asked my father for my hand in marriage. To my astonishment, my father looked at Jake and asked, "Do you plan on getting married in the church?"

Jake replied with a polite, "Yes, sir."

"Well, here's the deal. If you elope, I'll give you $500 and a ladder. But if you choose to get married in the church, you're on your own and I'll give you nothing."

At that, my calm and wise fiancé simply looked at my father. "Well, sir, we are planning on having a church wedding. Besides which, I already own a ladder!"

Six weeks following my twenty-second birthday, my father did walk me down the aisle. By then, it didn't matter to me whether his heart was in it; my attention was focused on my groom who waited for me at the altar. My wedding day was one of the most important days in my life.

I never understood my father's reasons for wanting us to elope—at least, not until many years later.

Our first several months on the farm were certainly an education for me, and for us as a couple. I adjusted to country living and he adjusted to living with a city girl. In many ways there were no differences, but there were times when we just didn't understand each other.

For example, whenever he left the farmyard, he'd tell me, "Now, make sure that you fill the tub and all of the pots with water if there's an electrical storm." I didn't ask why I needed to do this, because for whatever reason I had the notion that it was wrong to question my husband. Rather than seek an explanation, I lovingly did as he asked.

Eventually, however, the tension between my head, which questioned his instructions, and my heart, which wanted to support my husband, put me in a predicament.

One day while Jake was in town, a thunderstorm developed. He was concerned that the electricity would go out during the storm, so he called home.

"Fill the bathtub and all of the pots with water, okay?" he said.

"Okay! Sure thing!"

But I didn't do as he asked. Although I had responded in the affirmative, my inside voice said, *Yeah right.* I decided to do exactly the opposite of what he had requested.

When Jake came home from town, he came into the house only to find the bathtub completely empty. He entered the kitchen only to discover that the pots and the kettle were also bone dry.

"I don't understand," he calmly said, a bit frustrated. "I even called from town and asked you to fill up the bathtub and the pots with water. Why didn't you do it?"

By that point, I was understandably confused. But I was also concerned for my husband. Convinced that he had some phobia and that his only way to cope was to pour water into anything that could hold liquid, I lovingly asked him to sit down so we could talk.

Reluctantly and quizzically, he sat down and listened.

"Are you afraid of storms?" I asked.

Jake laughed at me. "Afraid of storms? Is that why you think we need to fill the tub with water?"

I felt somewhat hurt, because he continued laughing.

"Then tell me why we have to go through such a ritual," I said.

His explanation made me shake my head.

"It's not a ritual," he said. "You see, if the electricity goes out, then the pump, the one that pumps water out of the well into the house, can't work, and if the pump can't work, then we don't have any water to drink, or to wash dishes with, and so on."

It was as if a light came on.

"Ah! Okay, I see." Then it was my turn to explain. I walked over to the kitchen sink. "You see, Jake, when the electricity goes out in the city, we still have running water. We just turn the tap and, voila! Water!"

twenty-six

My Mother

DURING OUR SECOND YEAR OF MARRIAGE, JAKE AND I WERE BLESSED with our firstborn child, a daughter. Then, eighteen months later, we were blessed with a second daughter.

Being married to Jake gave me an overwhelming feeling of being loved. As I cherished him and began to understand the deep meaning of the love I had for him and my children, it occurred to me that I had never heard my mother tell me that she loved me.

In turn, I had never told my mother that I loved her. I felt an urgency in my spirit to tell her this before I missed the chance. So when she and my father were leaving our house one night, I hugged her and simply said, "Love ya!" To which she replied, "Love ya too!"

Little did I know that within a month's time we would be facing some very upsetting challenges.

twenty-seven

Sins of the Fathers

I TRIED TO READ MY BIBLE REGULARLY, BUT I STRUGGLED WITH understanding the Scriptures and their meaning. One particular verse seemed to go against my understanding of the God of love and justice I was getting to know: *"punishing the children for the sin of the parents to the third and fourth generation of those who hate me"* (Exodus 20:5).

The more I tried to balance the fairness of this verse, the more it bothered me. I wondered why I should be judged by the things my parents had done wrong while my friends, who had parents who were believers, were judged by what their parents had done right.

In order to obtain some clarification, I spoke to my pastor. The first thing he did was teach me a vital lesson in understanding the Bible.

"You cannot take the verse out of context," he said. "You have to keep reading. What does the next verse say?"

I opened my Bible and read the very next word: "But." Before I went on, he stopped me and explained that the word "but" gives us a way out—an alternative, so to speak—as well as a reason to pause and think. I continued reading the verse: *"but showing love to a thousand generations of those who love me and keep my commandments"* (Exodus 20:6).

He pointed out that *"[we] love because he first loved us"* (1 John 4:19). Then he explained that the reason we love God is because He loved us by sending His Son to die for us. Furthermore, it has been promised that His love shall abound for a thousand generations—not four, not five, but a thousand.

He then asked me to once again read Exodus 20:5, the verse that talks about the sin of the fathers. He explained that since we all have fathers who have sinned, we all face the consequences of both our own sins and theirs. He emphasized that what we face is the ramifications of those sins as opposed to the sins themselves.

"So whatever it is that your father, your parents, or even your grandparents have said or done, you and your siblings, your children, and maybe even your grandchildren will be affected by the consequences of those sins," my pastor said.

He encouraged me to do two things: to address the impacts of my father's actions on me and my children, and to continue loving God because His love abounds to me, my children, and the next generations.

Of course, I didn't yet know about my father's escapade to Florida and was therefore unaware of the consequences that might one day have for us. But I knew that no matter what my father had done, no matter what choices he had made, I could minimize the impact on my children and grandchildren simply by loving the Lord. My hope was that somehow, because of how I chose to live my life, my father's legacy on my children would be less than the legacy he had passed on to me.

My pastor went on to say, "Please remember: God has no grandchildren, only children."

He explained that we cannot pass down our love for Jesus. We can claim it and teach our children and grandchildren about it, but each of us has to come to our own understanding of God's love and receive His forgiveness of sins. Just as the next generation cannot inherit our Christian faith, the next generation cannot inherit eternal life; each person must choose this for themselves. And to those who do, Exodus 20:6 promises that He shows *"love to a thousand generations of those who love me and keep my commandments."*

Jesus answered him, "Truly I tell you, today you will be with me in paradise."

—Luke 23:43

twenty-eight

Healed

1981

MY SISTER ANNETTE AND I LOOKED QUIZZICALLY AT EACH OTHER when we arrived at our mother's hospital room to find the door closed.

When we stepped into her room, my mother wailed, "I have cancer!" Nothing can prepare a person's heart and mind to hear that diagnosis.

I sat on her bed and held her in my arms as she cried. My father sat on a chair in a state of shock. Apparently, a team of doctors had attended her room that morning and told her that the cancer surrounded her lungs and heart and had filled her abdominal cavity. Nothing more could be done.

My mother was so frightened. She knew that she had to fight to live at the same time that she felt physically unable to fight.

Several days later, my parents came to the farm to visit Jake and me and the girls. While she and I cleaned up after supper, she shared with me that she was struggling with whether there was life after death or whether life ended completely.

She recalled one of her fondest childhood memories about her father. "I loved hearing him preach," she said. Then, mimicking him, she added, "You must be born again!"

When she had been little, she'd asked Jesus to forgive her for her sins. She'd known that because of that decision, she would live with Him in heaven forever. But ever since, life had happened and her sins had accumulated. She now felt that she couldn't go to Jesus and ask Him for forgiveness because she'd committed too many sins to count.

Confronted with her own mortality, she was suddenly ready to make things right with God. She opted to write letters to televangelists, sending them money with a request that they pray for her to be healed.

When she finished sharing, I responded to her both attentively and lovingly. "Mom, I think it's awesome that you're asking God to heal you from this cancer. I want you to be healed too. But I am wondering something." I hesitated before continuing. "Is it possible that first and foremost God wants to heal your soul before He would heal your body?"

She listened intently as I explained to her that once we respond to Jesus's gift of salvation, there's a possibility that He will heal our body while we're still on earth, but there's a certainty that we will receive a whole new body when He takes us to heaven.

Next, I told her about heaven, quoting Revelation 21:4: *"He will wipe every tear from their eyes. There will be no more death or mourning or crying or pain..."* I then quoted from 1 John 1:9: *"If we confess our sins, he is faithful and just and will forgive us our sins and purify us from all unrighteousness."*

I reminded her that He forgives all of our sins, and all we have to do is believe in Him.

As I shared with her, I remembered thinking, *Wow! The message of the cross really is that simple. All we have to do is acknowledge our need for a Saviour, Jesus, confess our sins, and turn to Him.*

I didn't pressure her to do that, but I did say, "Take some time to think about it. Jesus is waiting for you, whenever you're ready."

We finished cleaning up the kitchen, then hugged each other good night.

That was one of the first true conversations I'd had with my mother that hadn't been influenced by alcohol on her part and a bad attitude on mine.

Once she started chemotherapy treatments, it seemed like her health started to improve. She was eating well and enjoying life more. Every little aspect of her life and surroundings seemed to be transformed. She even stopped by my kitchen one day to smell the bread baking. It was as if the colours of her life had been suddenly painted more brightly and beautiful than anyone else's. I wondered if that was natural for someone who had been told they would die soon. Or was it because my mother, like myself, hadn't taken the time to enjoy life's small wonders before this? Nevertheless, I was thrilled for her, and her new attitude influenced me greatly.

But within a very short period of time, she declined. She lost a lot of weight, lost strength daily, and deteriorated quickly. One day my father called and asked us children to meet him at the hospital. My mother had been hallucinating.

"Spiders!" he said. "She sees spiders everywhere! I think she might be having hallucinations due to withdrawing from the alcohol."

But given the length of time since she had stopped drinking, it was most likely that the hallucinations were from the drugs or the cancer, or possibly a combination of both.

We met my father at the hospital, where she had slipped into a coma. I sat by her bed for hours and listened as she tossed, turned, and cried out. Every so often she would open her eyes, look at me, and angrily say, "Why can't they leave me alone?" Then she would roll over and go back to sleep.

I didn't know who she was talking about, but I did know she was very angry. It was so difficult to see her like that; I went home that day feeling alone and very sad.

When I returned to the hospital the next day, she was sitting up in bed laughing. I was shocked, to say the least. She had rallied!

It was the beginning of a roller coaster. Over the next three weeks, I watched her slip in and out of consciousness. When she was awake, there were always people in and out of her room. When she was unconscious, she was angry.

She continued to grow weaker. First she lost the use of her legs, and then her breathing grew more difficult.

When the doctors asked my dad to call her children home, we gathered around her bed where we talked and prayed and sang and walked and shared with each other. We watched—we watched and waited for her to die.

After several days of being in a coma, my brother finally arrived home. He came to her side and said, "Hey, Mom. It's me, Stew!"

To our amazement, she immediately opened her eyes! It was as if she knew that this was the last child she hadn't yet seen and had somehow gathered enough strength to speak to him.

"Hi, Stew. How are you?"

Unaware that she hadn't spoken in days, he simply said, "Oh, I'm fine. It's you we're worried about." He paused. "Mom, I have only one question for you: where are you going when you die?"

"Well! I'm going to be with Jesus," she replied peacefully. "But you kids better pray for your father!"

Then she closed her eyes and slipped back into a coma. We all stood there with our mouths hanging open, totally amazed. She had made a commitment to Jesus and given clear verbal evidence of that commitment.

Over the next two days, we continued to be awed as we watched and waited. Jesus Christ had opened up heaven to her. She no longer cursed and fought; she no longer tossed and turned. Instead she verbalized amazement at what she saw. She said things like, "Wow! Awe! It's so beautiful!" Then she would say, "But not yet," followed by silence.

It would repeat several hours later, with her again expressing wonder and amazement over the beautiful things she'd seen and heard. A sense of peace would fill the room. Serenity would enshroud her face. Then once again she'd declare, "But not yet."

We don't know why she wasn't ready to go. Perhaps it was because she was so young, or perhaps there were things she still wanted to see and do on earth. Yet as her body gave way to the disease, she continued to reveal beautiful things to us about heaven.

I was reminded of Stephen in the book of Acts. He had just finished giving his speech to the Sanhedrin about the faith of Abraham and Moses, warning the people about being so stiff-necked. The Sanhedrin was furious with him.

But Stephen, full of the Holy Spirit, looked up to heaven and saw the glory of God, and Jesus standing at the right hand of God.

"Look," he said, "I see heaven open and the Son of Man standing at the right hand of God."

*At this they covered their ears and, yelling at the top of their
voices, they all rushed at him, dragged him out of the city and began
to stone him.*

—Acts 7:55–58

How amazing it is to think that two thousand years after God
opened heaven up to Stephen, He also opened heaven up to my mother.

Two days later, my mother took her last breaths and Jesus took her
home. At her request, my father arranged for one of the elders from our
Sunday school to officiate at the funeral. There, he shared the story from
the Gospel of Luke about the thief on the cross and how, in his last moment, with his last waking breath, he had said, *"Jesus, remember me when
you come into your kingdom"* (Luke 23:42). And Jesus had answered, *"I tell
you the truth, today you will be with me in paradise"* (Luke 23:43).

We knew, without a doubt, that my mother had gone to live with
Jesus in paradise.

Immediately following her death, the hospital conducted an autopsy.
Many months later, the doctors met with us and basically said, "We don't
know what to tell you. The autopsy revealed that there was no cancer. Every tumour we removed and every test we did when she was alive directed
us to our diagnosis of cancer, but the autopsy showed that there was no
cancer. As a result, we have listed the reason for her death as pneumonia."

My brothers and sisters expressed a mixture of emotions.

Lord, that is so like You, I thought. *You answered her prayer to heal her.
At her very last breath, when she was dying, You not only took her soul and
healed it through the power of your shed blood, but You took her body and You
healed that too.*

I will see her again.

twenty-nine

David and Doreen

I first met Doreen at my mother's funeral visitation. It was apparent that David was very happy and in love with her. She was bubbly and seemed sincere.

Aunt Victoria passed away a few years after my mother. David had a very difficult time with the loss of his mother and later told me that even though he loved her, deep down he wished things could have been different between them. He wished she could have protected him when he was a child.

Nevertheless, despite those difficult childhood years, David was determined that his role as a husband and father was going to be different. He and Doreen were blessed with four children, he had a great job, and Doreen had a managerial position with a cosmetics company.

David created a lot of fun with his chosen family; he was very spontaneous and enjoyed the thrill that came from being impulsive. On one occasion, he and Doreen drove to the west coast of Canada just for the fun of it. Fortunately, Doreen was wired the same way and was just fine when he called her up and told her to have a bag ready because they were going away for a few days. David admitted that some of this spontaneity came from being in foster care, while some of it came from his mother dropping him off at a variety of people's homes. Some of it just came naturally.

During the early years of their marriage, Doreen and David were invited to church by some neighbours. They initially attended as a family, but after a while David's attendance trailed off. Since Doreen took the children on a regular basis, though, David occasionally attended with her.

One evening when he was home alone, David realized how deeply he had been influenced by Doreen's dedication to the Lord as well as to him and their children. At that moment, his life and all of its rough spots had been set on a collision course with his faith.

With the prodding of the Holy Spirit, David rededicated his life fully to the Lord. He got on his knees and said, "Father, I'm sorry for the things I've done wrong. I know You died on the cross to forgive me for my sins. And Lord, I'm sorry that I've gone astray and not kept my eyes on You. Please forgive me for that as well. Please walk with me now as I seek to serve You and my family."

Sometime later, David shared with Doreen what he had prayed. Doreen rejoiced! They once again attended church together. He was later baptized on confession of his faith in Jesus Christ. After that, he was determined to make changes so that he could live a whole and honouring life to God, his wife, and his family.

Life was awesome!

If I say, "Surely the darkness will hide me and the light become night around me," even the darkness will not be dark to you; the night will shine like the day, for darkness is as light to you.

—Psalm 139:11–12

thirty

Darkness Turns to Despair

1994

I WAS THRILLED TO BE JAKE'S WIFE AND THOROUGHLY ENJOYED BEING a mother to our three daughters. Our love for each other and our home life was built on the love of Christ. We attended church, prayed, and did devotions together, all in an effort to grow closer to the Lord and teach our children about Jesus and His love.

I learned how to cook, sew, and even drive a tractor! I was involved in our children's lives, taught Sunday school, and volunteered at their school. I loved writing poetry and spent time writing whenever I had a chance. In addition, I took university courses, completing one course at a time, determined that I would put my stubbornness towards something positive. I established a goal to complete my degree, and then I aimed for it. Life was busy!

I missed my mother incredibly, especially since we had started to connect with each other at the end of her life. I felt cheated by this loss. But my mother had always said, "Life goes on!"

Life had gone on.

I was living a new normal, and it was good.

❧

Before long, thirteen years had passed since losing my mother, during which time I relied on the rhythms of each day. There were many things on which I could depend, including Jake's love and Jesus's love: the sun rising, the moon setting, hearts beating, the seasons coming and going, and the waters lapping the shore then going out and returning once more.

Most days started out with the same daily routine. I would rise, shower, dress, eat, make lunches, and go to work. Step by step, I went through these automatic movements without thought. Many events returned to my calendar year after year, such as celebrations and holidays that each provided a sense of the known, the expected, and even the expectant.

On one beautiful spring day, the sky was blue, bright, and sunny.

I rejoiced that I had been blessed with three beautiful daughters— then nine, thirteen, and nearly fifteen. As they got ready for school, I marveled at how different their childhoods were from how mine had been, especially when I'd been fifteen.

It was such a joy to raise my children in the country. I realized that I was growing up all over again with them. I put the girls on their school bus, waved goodbye, and then headed to work, seemingly without a care in the world. I listened to the radio as I drove.

Suddenly, an image flashed before my eyes. It was a memory of me as a little girl, climbing stairs while holding a man's hand. It felt as if I had been transported back in time to a place I vaguely remembered yet hadn't thought about for a very long time. Though I was totally aware of driving my vehicle, I felt both emotionally and physically present somewhere else. It was the strangest sensation. Fear engulfed me and I burst into tears.

I chose to keep this mini mental breakdown to myself.

Approximately two weeks later, while driving to the grocery store, I was struck with the same bizarre experience and recalled the exact same memory. As before, it came out of the blue and without warning. But this time I saw more details. For example, I remembered standing with the man at the top of the stairs. I felt afraid and rattled and knew that I would have to physically shake it off. I tucked the experience away, unwilling and unable to talk to anyone about it.

Over the next several months, I had the same dream over and over again, night after night. In it I was aware that there was an extra bedroom somewhere in my house and I would wander through the house looking for the door to this bedroom, even checking at the back of each closet, all in effort to find my way to that bedroom.

The dream was so vivid and felt so real that it even haunted me during the day. I would wander around my own house to see whether there were extra rooms we hadn't yet discovered.

Over time, the dreams intensified and provided more detail. In the dream, I eventually found the door to the bedroom. When I opened it, a bed sat in the middle of an otherwise empty room, but I also sensed the terrifying presence of evil and wickedness.

Again, I was unwilling and unable to talk to anyone about it. I shrugged it off and tucked my fears away in the back of my mind, busying myself with my work, chores, and my roles as wife and mother.

I felt like I had lost my mind.

As time progressed, I got very little sleep and felt like I was functioning on pure adrenalin. My ability to cope with normal difficulties in our lives diminished. I was scared to tell anyone about what was happening in my head, though, because I was worried they would think I was nuts. I had well-remembered Aunt Victoria's poor mental health and now I was worried about my own.

I began to plead with God. "Lord, please. Please don't let me lose my mind."

I felt a weight bearing down on me, like a physical burden that was too heavy to carry. Soon the heaviness surrounded me like thick fog, lasting from daybreak until the darkness of night. It removed any sense of hope, and I felt myself slip deeper into insignificance. Beaten down, I felt defeated and couldn't seem to find a way to shake it off. I was scared, anxious, and distressed.

The darkness had seemingly come out of nowhere. I felt like I had fallen into a pit where there was no bottom. The darkness blanketed my world and prevented any light from filtering through. I felt incredibly sad. I woke up early every morning and was unable to get back to sleep. I cried all the time, without limits and sometimes without reason. There was no relief from the images that came into my head, no reprieve from the emotional pain that tormented me.

One morning, I awoke with a start as I remembered the room in more vivid detail: the wallpaper, the closet, the bed, and what had happened to me there. Despite my awareness of lying in bed next to my husband, I felt as though I was transported to that room in my memory. I was very confused. The sensation was so real, so vivid, that it really did seem like I was in two places at once.

Somehow the two worlds merged together so that I couldn't understand why my husband wasn't doing anything to stop it… why my husband wasn't doing anything to stop *him*. I couldn't understand why my husband couldn't hear me gasp for air as I tried to scream. I felt so angry—angry at what was happening to me and angry at my husband *who just kept on sleeping.*

I checked myself to make sure I was awake and not sleeping. I wasn't having a dream. I was awake and it felt all too real. In fact, it felt like it was actually happening to me all over again, just as it had happened more than thirty years ago.

Without saying anything, and in an effort to conceal this ludicrous fracture in my thinking, I somehow managed to get out of bed and get ready for my day. But when my friend saw me later than morning, still visibly shaken, I confided a few things to her.

"You need to see a psychiatrist!" she told me.

I knew that I needed to talk to someone and felt there was no other option but to seek out a counsellor. The pastor at the new church we were attending also had a counselling degree, and I had seen him on a few occasions to talk about the distress I'd been under since leaving our former church. Feeling so broken down, I called him and made an appointment.

During that appointment, with tears streaming down my face, I shared with him, "When I was younger, there was a man who violated me." Suddenly, I no longer felt like a thirty-eight-year-old woman. Rather, I felt like I was six years old again.

In another almost out-of-body experience, I watched myself as I sat in the chair in the pastor's office. I grabbed my knees, pulled them up to my chest, and rocked back and forth in an effort to comfort myself.

After sharing a few things about my life, I looked up and I saw the pastor wipe a tear off his cheek. Other than my husband, no one had ever shown me that kind of consideration or compassion.

My pastor encouraged me to tell Jake about the nightmare I'd been living the previous five months. At first I felt nervous about Jake's reaction, but then I recalled that he had already supported me through some of my father's inappropriate behaviours. For example, when I had been expecting my third child, my father had greeted me at a family get-together in an extremely improper way. I had taken him to task, letting him know that he was never to do that to me again. I was so angry at him! It was something I had seen him do to women in the past, and it had always disgusted me. I was appalled that he would cross that line with his own daughter.

Jake hadn't witnessed the incident, but I later made him aware of what had happened and how it had affected me. Any thread of trust between my father, Jake, and me had been completely broken that day.

Even though Jake knew about the incident, I still worried about what his reaction would be once he heard about what my father had done to me as a child. But then I remembered an experience Jake had had in church a few weeks earlier. During a Sunday morning worship service, while the congregation was singing, Jake had experienced a strong encounter with the Holy Spirit. Tears had flooded his eyes at the same time that his heart was inundated with joy and gratitude for the awesome power of the Spirit. He had been showered with the gift of faith, which reaffirmed in him that the walk in life he had chosen—the Christian walk—was the right one.

Remembering this, I knew in my heart that God had already prepared Jake for the difficulties I'd had to deal with.

Later that evening, while our children were sleeping, I found the courage to share with Jake what I had been experiencing and about my father's offenses against me. Jake wasn't surprised. He just held me close, let me cry, and told me that he loved me. Amazingly, over the next several months Jake's renewed faith in Jesus allowed him to love and support me, pray for me, and be patient with me as he walked alongside me as any best friend would.

But inside I felt unworthy of Jake and his love. I felt dirty and ashamed, used and abused. I thought that he would think less of me than he had before, because I thought less of me. I had no desire for any intimate connection with him, and I even pushed away his attempts at deepening our emotional relationship. When he told me that he loved me, I put him down. After all, in my mind I wasn't loveable. How could he possibly love me!?

Over the next several months, I grieved over my childhood and what had happened. I ached physically and emotionally. As more memories came to the forefront of my mind, they tipped me into a sinister and evil place, into a deep pit of depression where darkness turned into despair. Tears flowed freely and frequently.

Although the darkness seemed to have come suddenly, I recognized that it had been draping its cloak of heaviness over me for years. But I had done a good job of running away from it, of covering it up and ignoring it. I'd thought I could handle troubles as they came my way. I'd thought I could move on and create the life I'd dreamed about ever since the age of fifteen.

The problem was that I really hadn't handled the emotional pressures in my life; I had hidden them, put them under the front porch with me, tucked them into the back of the closet, into the corner of the doghouse.

I had hidden them in the closet of my mind.

I felt so lost and didn't know which way to turn. There were times when I so badly wanted to ask for prayer, but that would have meant explaining to people what I was going through. Since that wasn't an option, I merely kept quiet.

I soon found a small group of people who were trustworthy and wouldn't talk to anyone about these dark things. They became my life source as they prayed for me and often called me just to say they cared about me and loved me.

The Scriptures also gave me comfort and peace.

thirty-one

In the Pit with Darkness

I REALIZED THAT I COULDN'T PHYSICALLY RUN AWAY FROM THIS emotional pain, so I seized the pain and trapped it into the attic of my mind. Since darkness loomed there, I fumbled to find a place to hide from the torment and pain. There was no place to run, no place to hide.

When I was alone, I screamed and yelled and cried. Tears flowed freely and drowned me in a sea of hurt. But when I was with people, my heart screamed out. I cried on the inside but smiled on the outside.

It had only taken one thought to throw me into that pit of darkness, a thought that had stayed with me as far back as I could remember: "Nobody loves me. Everybody hates me."

Immediately prior to remembering the childhood abuse, someone had made a very hurtful statement to me regarding my cultural background. I interpreted that statement to mean I didn't belong. The pain of that comment may have triggered the same emotions I had stored in my memory at the time of the sexual abuse. Those same intense feelings of not belonging, of being in the way, and of being unloved and unwanted may have resulted in the memories rising to the surface. It's also possible that the memories of the sexual abuse had been triggered when I thought about my oldest daughter turning fifteen and recognized how very difficult my fifteenth year had been.

Regardless, the emotions I faced brought with them the most horrendous, vicious, and horrible memories from my childhood. They reinforced my memory of hiding under the front porch of our house when I was six years old, crying my eyes out. Darkness had been part of my life then, at a time when my face had been smothered under the weight of *his* body and I had been forced to see only the chilling blackness. Darkness had been part of my life when my mother had discovered that my father had offended me at night-time. Rather than yell at him about the inappropriateness of his deed, she had made it an issue that I shouldn't be in their bedroom. She had made me the problem, rather than him and what he had done to me.

Over the next couple of months, I remembered more about my childhood. I remembered climbing the stairs of my uncle's house, holding the hand of a man and being petrified. In my thirty-eight-year-old mind, I didn't want to go to the top of the stairs, but in my six-year-old mind I had no fear and kept climbing those stairs because I trusted the man who walked with me.

One morning, I remembered everything that had happened to me when I got to the top of those stairs. I had wanted to play with toys, but the man had kept telling me it was bedtime. It was still light outside, it was summertime, and I didn't want to go into that bedroom. I didn't want to go! I kicked him. I was afraid of him. He picked me up and threw me onto the bed. I looked over at the closet, wishing I could hide in there, I needed somewhere to hide, I needed somewhere to go, I knew that downstairs my mother and the others were playing cards and drinking, I knew they were totally oblivious to the pain I had just suffered.

I was very confused. After all, I was married with three beautiful children who embraced me with open arms and told me they loved me. My husband often told me he loved me. But I was daily faced with the dichotomy of hearing that I was loved while my child's heart felt so unloved.

My faith was shaken when I came to believe that even God couldn't love me. The more I believed I was unloved by others and by God, the darker my thoughts and feelings about myself grew, which caused my pain to retreat deeper into the fissures and crevices of my mind. The deeper my pain travelled, the darker my world got, to the point where the light became night.

If I say, "Surely the darkness will hide me and the light become night around me..."

—Psalm 139:11

When the night set in, there was no light and hope was lost. Darkness had done his job.

Before a word is on my tongue you, Lord, know it completely.

—Psalm 139:4

If only you, God, would slay the wicked! Away from me, you who are bloodthirsty!

—Psalm 139:19

thirty-two

Changing the Lies to the Truth

I ATTENDED COUNSELLING FOR SEVERAL MONTHS. I SHARED ABOUT the abuse, sorted through the memories, and agonized over the emotional pain.

"We can't do anything at this point in time to change what your father did to you," my pastor repeatedly told me. "What he did to you was wrong and it is very normal for you to feel the way you do. It's normal for you to feel angry. It's important that you separate the lies from the truth. Satan is the father of lies and he will try to get you to believe a lot of negative things about yourself. Look for the truth about yourself and replace those negative thoughts and feelings with the truth."

He then emphasized his point by suggesting that as soon as I had any negative thoughts about myself I replace them with positive and truthful thoughts about myself. More importantly, he encouraged me to change them to thoughts based on the truths of Scripture.

In my daily Bible reading, I came across a verse in the Psalms one day: *"Record my misery; list my tears on your scroll—are they not in your record?"* (Psalm 56:8) Another translation puts it this way: *"You keep track of all my sorrows. You have collected all my tears in your bottle. You have recorded each one in your book."* (Psalm 56:8 NLT)

I was blown away when I realized that God cared so much about me that He even recorded each and every one of my tears as it fell. In order to personalize the meaning of this verse, I imagined a bottle sitting at the feet of Jesus. Then I watched as He counted my tears as they fell into the bottle. In my imagination, I tried to hear each individual tear as it landed. *Plunk, plunk, plunk, plunk...*

I cried; God counted.

Plunk, plunk, plunk, plunk.

At the time when the abuse happened, I was obviously too little to understand what my father had done to me. But I clearly recalled my mother walking into the room, and instead of yelling at him about what she saw him doing, she yelled about me being in their bedroom. I have always remembered her screaming, "She shouldn't be in our room!"

Of course, I processed that to mean it was my fault because I was in the way. I blamed myself; if the house had been bigger, I wouldn't have been sleeping in their room. That overall feeling of being a nuisance always stayed with me.

Through processing these habitual thoughts, I was confronted with the realization that the responsibility to keep me safe clearly lay with the adults in my life. Furthermore, the size of the house in which we lived didn't give my father license to do what he did. In addition, my being in their bedroom clearly was not the problem; the problem was that he did something extremely inappropriate. What he did to me was wrong!

Plunk, plunk, plunk, plunk.

I had always been a loving child and enjoyed all the attention I could get, whether through mischievous behaviours or by sitting on someone's lap for a cuddle or two. As a result, I felt that because of my need to be loved, I had encouraged the abuse, that I had somehow asked for it.

One of the hardest things for me to understand was what happened to me physiologically. From my best recollection, although what my father did to me was extremely terrifying, my body reacted to the stimulation. This left me believing that I was somehow a sicko for having "enjoyed" it. The combination of my physiological reaction and believing I had led him on made me feel very negative about myself. When I understood that I didn't have the ability to control my body's physical reactions and that I wasn't responsible for my father's actions, I was able to be less self-critical.

Plunk, plunk, plunk, plunk.

My father often stipulated that children were a curse, the unfortunate end result of having sex. Since I was the youngest, I interpreted that to mean that my family would have been better off if I hadn't been born, because then there would have been more money available for the others.

My pastor pointed me to Jesus and His love and provision for me: *"From birth I have relied on you; you brought me forth from my mother's womb"* (Psalm 71:6) and *"even the very hairs of your head are all numbered"* (Matthew 10:30).

These truths from Scripture challenged me to change my thinking about my sense of worth. I started to recognize that God had been involved from the very beginning of my existence.

Plunk, plunk, plunk, plunk.

As a child, and even as a teenager, I was always embarrassed by my father. As much as I loved him and loved to be with him, I often felt humiliated when I was with him because he would make vulgar and smutty comments to people he met. In addition, there was a barrage of lewd comments and sexualized jokes in our home, some of which were directed towards me. I often felt mortified and ashamed of myself because of those statements. For example, when I was twelve I wore an oversized sweatshirt for most of the summer due to the shame I felt from my father's thoughtless and offensive reference to my developing body.

I also became aware that I needed to come to terms with the shame I felt because of the family to which I belonged. My heart longed to be able to proudly say, "I am the daughter of ..." or "My father is..." Even as a child, whenever anyone would ask me about my family or my roots, my insides would cringe. I was incessantly teased at school not because I was stupid or ugly, but because of my family name. Kids would gather on the schoolyard, point at me, and mockingly sing out my family name.

As an adult, I no longer wanted my identity to be tied to my father. I was fully aware that people could tell I was my father's daughter from my looks and mannerisms. Inasmuch as I reflected my father in public, when my father screwed up, it also reflected back on me. In this shame, I floundered and found it difficult to find a solid footing to stand as my own individual self.

Through counselling, I started to recognize that I wasn't responsible for my parents or their actions and began to release the shame I felt.

Plunk, plunk, plunk, plunk.

One of my biggest struggles was how I felt about God. I wrestled with the question "How can a true and loving God love me yet let those things happen to me?" I envisioned God as He looked down from heaven and watched as my father abused me. At times my anger towards God was intense and I would shake my fist at Him and scream.

My pastor explained to me that God can have nothing to do with evil and noted that when Jesus was crucified on the cross, He cried out, *"My God, my God, why have you forsaken me?"* (Matthew 27:46) God didn't turn His back on Jesus; rather, He turned His back on the evil that Jesus took on Himself as He bore the sins of the world. My pastor also explained that God had no part in the evil committed against me. However, because we live in a sinful world, evil and sinful things do happen and will happen. Once again, he reminded me that because God is love, He loved me then, continued to love me, and He will always love me.

I tried to understand this without fully seeing the bigger picture.

Plunk, plunk, plunk, plunk.

Anger took on a life of its own within me. I was so angry—angry at my father, my parents, my family, myself, and at times the whole world! I was angry at myself because I hadn't remembered the abuse before I got married. I felt that this hadn't been fair to Jake. Because I saw myself as marred, I was convinced that Jake also saw me as marred, even though he told me repeatedly that he didn't see me that way.

Plunk, plunk, plunk, plunk.

I became aware that people call it abuse for a reason.

The tears fell. God counted.

Plunk, plunk, plunk, plunk.

thirty-three

The Triggers

THE MEMORIES WERE SO VIVID THAT IT FELT LIKE I WAS ACTUALLY reliving the events while living in the present. At times it felt like I was having an out-of-body experience, as though my emotions and spirit were separate from my body and frantically trying to find somewhere to go, somewhere to hide, somewhere to feel safe.

These unsettling and frightening experiences were often triggered by a bang, or a sound, or sometimes a smell. In particular, the smell of beer mixed with cigarettes and some men's colognes caused me to feel unsafe, shaky, and anxious. Other times, if I was approached by someone wearing all black or if I found myself in a crowded situation, I would want to run away or curl up and hide.

These triggers put me in uncomfortable social situations. At times they caused me to emotionally check out of conversations. Although I could hear the conversations around me, I was unable to participate; my body would remain motionless, frozen to the spot. During other intense emotional moments, I was able to physically walk away from people.

When some people heard about the issues from my childhood, they wanted to share their own experiences of incest. Although I was open to listening to them, the triggers were at times so intense during our discussions that I had to protect myself by changing the conversation. Unfortunately, this left some people feeling unsupported.

On one occasion, Jake and I were on an outing with the children and we were asked to sit in the back seat of another person's vehicle. I got in first and then Jake joined me. But as he crawled into the back seat next to me, my insides started to shake, my hands began to sweat, and I felt dizzy. I screamed and tried frantically to get out of the vehicle. Jake's black coat had triggered a memory of when my father had abused me; I recalled pitch darkness, like a large black ball bearing down on me. We rectified the effects of that trigger by Jake simply and lovingly removing his black coat.

I hated the triggers and how they made me feel, and it always took time for me to recover from them. I found ways to relax and calm down, usually through prayer, so that I could restore myself to a calm place once again. But I also became hypervigilant about many things. For example, if there was a group of men standing together talking after church, rather than try to go around them, in fear that I might touch one of them, I would go out the front door of the church and then re-enter through the back door. If we went into a restaurant, I would always sit at the table with my back to the bar.

Although there were times when I felt like all my little quirks got in the way of living, when I became proactive Jake would partner with me in helping me get through situations as best I could. Truly, he has been the best husband for me.

thirty-four

A Hug from Jesus

As I continued to address the childhood abuse, I clearly saw ways in which the Lord Jesus had intervened for me, and I was always amazed at the lengths He went to in order to support me and show me how much He loved me.

One particular day, I was under incredible stress at work closing real estate deals. I headed to the bank at mid-afternoon, and on the way there I listened to a taped message which concentrated on the things we can do to stay close to the Lord Jesus. As I pulled into the parking lot, the preacher was closing his message with a prayer. I wanted to stay in my car in order to listen to the end of the prayer, but I noticed several people entering the bank. Since time was of the essence, I decided to park my car and head inside to stand in line with the others.

It was a beautiful spring day. The sky was blue and the air smelled fresh after a soft spring shower. Everyone in the bank appeared to be in a jolly mood; they talked and laughed as they waited in line.

Then it happened. I saw him—a man with a similar physique to my father, heavyset and balding. He started to make his way down the row of waiting people, making merry and hugging everyone as he went. My heart started to beat hard and fast; it felt like it was literally going to explode out of my chest. This man's size, his outgoing personality, and his flirtatious demeanour reminded me of my father and triggered a sense of fear in me.

As my heart raced, I felt lightheaded and sweaty. My thoughts told me I was fine, but my emotions told me that I wasn't safe and that I should leave.

I didn't want to hug this man. In fact, I didn't want to hug *any* man. I struggled with my conflicted feelings of wanting to be polite at the same time as I wanted to hit the guy! All of these thoughts and feelings fired through me while I watched him approach. When he stopped in front of me, I put out my hand to greet him.

"Ahhh," he said insistently, holding out his wide open arms. "Let me give you a hug!"

"I don't want a hug," I said as quickly and friendly as I could. "But I'll shake your hand."

A little more persistent, he again extended his arms. He stepped a bit closer and said, louder, "Let me give you a hug!"

Once again I told him that I didn't want his hug, but I would shake his hand.

Everyone in the bank now seemed to have their eyes fixed on this altercation between the jolly man and the not-so-jolly woman who didn't want his hug. The tellers stopped working, the managers stood and watched, and the people in line waited to see how this would play out.

"Aw, hug the man," the lady immediately in front of me said.

Her words cut through my soul. My legs shook as I again held out my hand.

"I don't want a hug," I said once again, in an attempt to be polite. "But I'll shake your hand."

The man, his ego a little bruised, finally shook my hand and made his way back up the line, hugging everyone again as he went. The tellers went back to work and the customers returned to their laughing and joking.

As for me, I stood there crying in the middle of the bank. I wanted so badly to feel normal and to be able to just hug a strange, friendly, unassuming man who had likely meant no harm. I wanted to have the ability to laugh it off as if it meant nothing. I wanted so badly to run out of the bank, but I had a deposit to make and didn't have time to come back in and line up again!

So I stood there and cried. With tears streaming down my face, the teller patiently and quietly waited on me while I tried signing my name.

I finished my business, then returned to my car, hoping not to meet up with the jolly man in the parking lot.

That's when it happened.

As I drove away, I resumed listening to the cassette tape of the pastor's prayer: "Dear Jesus, please reach your loving arms down from heaven and give your child a big hug. Amen."

I was hugged by Jesus—and I have been hugged by Jesus on many days since! In the midst of a world that doesn't understand me, I can rest safe and secure in His loving arms.

Cast all your anxiety on him because he cares for you.
—1 Peter 5:7

Before a word is on my tongue you, Lord, know it completely.

—Psalm 139:4

thirty-five

Darkness's Cousin: Anger

WHEN I WAS A CHILD, I ANGERED EASILY. WHEN THINGS DIDN'T GO my way, I stomped my feet, yelled, and demanded until I got what I wanted. The combination of a very short fuse and a stubborn will resulted in behaviours that were so out of control that my parents and siblings nicknamed me their "banty rooster."

As I grew older and more mature, I learned how to control anger, but it always felt like anger simmered just below the surface.

Then, once I started to address my childhood pain, anger erupted. At times it was a low rumble. Other times, anger spewed venom and vengeance. I sometimes ranted and raved like a madwoman over the littlest things. I became demanding, a yeller, and a cupboard door banger.

When I realized that these rants affected my children, rather than find appropriate ways to articulate my anger, I turned it inward and buried it deep inside. I believe that's when anger and darkness teamed up in an attempt to find a secret place in my spirit. My unresolved anger was so intense in my spirit that it created pressure in my chest, a constant knot and feeling of tightness that wouldn't go away.

I knew deep down that my anger needed to be directed at my father, but since he was in a nursing home and had become a frail and forgetful old man, I didn't know how to do that. So I once again turned the anger inward by imagining acts of torture that I felt needed to be done to him so he could no longer feel again as a man.

I was extremely angry at myself. Self-hatred was boiling inside because of my inability to accept myself.

Although I had begun to understand that God wasn't responsible for what had happened to me—after all, He can have nothing to do with evil—I was unable to find healthy ways to vent my anger. I felt like my only recourse was to yell and scream at Him. This inappropriate placement of my anger was so intense that it blinded me from seeing the love He had for me. My anger fuelled the lie that He'd closed His eyes when I was abused and allowed it to happen. This affected my relationship with Him, as I couldn't grasp how a loving God could have allowed such an evil act in my life.

Even though I knew I was entitled to my feelings and that it was okay to feel angry, I also knew that I needed to do the right thing when I expressed anger. As Paul reminded the Ephesians, *"In your anger do not sin"* (Ephesians 4:26).

"You know, God was angry when you were abused," a friend once told me. "He cried. He cries for all His children. He didn't make man to sin. He gets very angry every time His babies are hurt. You are still His precious baby, His little girl! In His presence, there is healing and restoration. Spend time in His presence and you will see His healing power. God is working harder than you for your freedom. Go ahead and scream! It's good to let it out. Vomit up the anger until you're purged. Only He can truly begin to fill you with love. You are a precious sister in the Lord."

Scream I did! I went to the barn and screamed. I threw things and screamed. I screamed when I was alone in the car. I screamed at inanimate objects. I even screamed at my pillow! All in an attempt to vomit up anger.

But there was so much anger.

And anger had its hold on me.

thirty-six

Rays of Light

Somewhere, somehow, in the middle of my madness, illuminating experiences beamed down like rays of light between the clouds of darkness, times when I was able to say that despite the bad, there was good.

One day, while helping Jake clean up pieces of scrap metal for recycling, I came across a short length of chain. I tossed it aside until I came across a few more short lengths. From their size and shape, it was apparent that the links had once been connected. While I examined the pieces, I was reminded of a verse in the book of Acts: *"Suddenly an angel of the Lord appeared and a light shone in the cell. He struck Peter on the side and woke him up. "Quick, get up!" he said, and the chains fell off Peter's wrists"* (Acts 12:7).

I could only imagine what it must have been like for Peter to be suddenly released from the chains that had bound him.

Then it struck me that even though I had been tied down by the chains of abuse, I was being set free from that bondage. When I later shared this insight with my pastor, he pointed out that by being protective of my children I had freed them from chains of abuse that could have bound them.

My deep love for my daughters meant that I would do anything to protect them. But this longing became a balancing act for me. On the one hand, I wanted to go with them everywhere, always ready to glare at or pounce on a potential violator. But on the other hand, I had to learn to control my anxiety long enough to allow them to be kids, to learn to protect themselves, speak up for themselves, and recognize for themselves that there was good and evil in the world.

Even though I hadn't remembered the early childhood sexual abuse until the girls were older, I had always been fully aware of my father's sexually heightened character, including his inappropriate comments, jokes, and lewd remarks. These were enough to make me wary of my girls being around my father.

Our children knew that they were loved unconditionally, that our love for them was based on who they were as people and not on what they did. They knew there was nothing they could do that would stop us from loving them. They also understood that they needed to love others unconditionally.

I struggled with the conflict between hating what my father had done while knowing that I was to love who he was as a person. This conflict, the one between our need to love others unconditionally and our need to protect our girls, posed difficulties. We wanted to give our children reasons to be wary of him, but we also wanted them to respect their grandfather.

As a result, without telling them the reasons for my concern, we prioritized safety first, and then love. We ended up having minimal contact with him. The distance between the inner city and our rural setting worked to our advantage, as it meant the girls only saw their grandfather when I was present; they were never left alone with him. We also developed a secret code word, and the girls knew that a person was only considered safe if he used the right word. Of course, we never told my father about this word.

Knowing that I was breaking the chains of abuse became a bright ray of hope which I could hold on to as I continued to fight for healing and cry out to the Lord, asking Him to save me from my suffering.

Then they cried to the Lord in their trouble, and he saved them from their distress. He brought them out of darkness, the utter darkness, and broke away their chains. Let them give thanks to the Lord for his unfailing love and his wonderful deeds for mankind...
—Psalm 107:13–15

thirty-seven

My Identity in Christ

WHILE DARKNESS, ANGER, TEARS, AND THE TRIGGERS ENCROACHED on me, I fought against them and tried to get stronger, both emotionally and spiritually. But it was a constant battle.

One day, my little great niece approached me at a family get-together, wondering who I was. In her own two-year-old vernacular, she asked, "Who am you?"

I thought that was so adorable! But I also thought her question was insightful. As a society, we never ask people who they "am"; we're usually more interested in what they do. When asked who they are, people tend to answer with their name or the relationship they have to another person or place. Ideally, however, it would be nice if this question could also be seen to inquire about the depths of a person—that is, their inner qualities and characteristics.

This little one's question made me realize that I never truly answer this question beyond an external description of myself. It also made me wonder whether I too should be asking people, as she did, "Who am you?"

I was aware that I could, from my outward physical traits, describe myself in ways that make me distinct from anyone else: I am female with green eyes, dark brown hair, and crooked teeth. Those things identify me on the outside. I even carry some identification that provides details like my address, weight, and height.

But her question made me realize that I didn't know for certain who I was on the inside. Apart from my outward characteristics, what did I truly believe about myself?

My pastor once challenged me by asking, "What do you believe about yourself?" I have to admit that my response was one of negativity. Although I could mention some of my successes, capabilities, and qualities, I couldn't say any of it with certainty. In fact, I wasn't even certain that I believed they existed or were important. When I identified a good quality about myself, I made a negative comment to refute it.

But when it came to the very core of my being, the very heart of my soul, I was incapable of seeing myself as loved because I didn't see myself as loveable. I was unable to see myself as valued because I didn't see myself as valuable. I was unable to see myself as cared for because I saw myself as scarred, marred, broken, used, and abused.

These thoughts overwhelmed my ability to see the true extent of who I was as a person, and they resulted in me not caring about myself or valuing or loving myself. My inability to understand my true identity may have also contributed to my depression.

With my pastor's assistance, I started to understand that my perception of my self-worth was distorted, and for the most part grounded on the wrong things. I had based my self-worth on my accomplishments, abilities, and strengths rather than on my true essence. Although those things helped define who I was as a person, they did not in themselves prescribe value or worth.

In fact, when I looked closely at those things, I discovered that they could be easily retracted, especially my abilities. For example, I had played clarinet in high school. Because I'd believed I was exceptionally good, I had placed part of my self-worth on that ability. But when I stopped practicing and lost the ability to play well, my self-worth teeter-tottered.

Through many deep conversations with my pastor, I began to realize the importance of ensuring that my identity, my worth as person, was fixed on something solid, on something that couldn't be moved or shaken.

My pastor suggested that I might consider the importance of placing my identity in Jesus Christ in order to see myself as God sees me, as He really sees me, in spite of my background, family, difficulties, or the things that had happened to me. Because He never changes, my self-worth would always be grounded on something solid: *"Jesus Christ is the same yesterday and today and forever*" (Hebrews 13:8). It therefore made perfect sense to place my identity in Him.

As I began to understand who I was in Christ Jesus, I was humbled to realize that God, God Almighty, Sovereign God, had a very different view of me than I had of myself!

I uncovered Psalm 139:13–14: "*For you created my inmost being; you knit me together in my mother's womb. I praise you because I am fearfully and wonderfully made; your works are wonderful, I know that full well.*" God made me. Every fibre, bone, and drop of blood that produced me was woven together by the very hands of God.

> *Before I formed you in the womb I knew you, before you were born I set you apart.*
>
> —Jeremiah 1:5

I began to realize that not only had God created me, but He'd planned me. I considered the amount of planning that goes into developing a subdivision, including the drawings that show roads, parks, and lots for houses. Those plans are carefully laid out. Likewise, God had a plan for me: "'For I know the plans I have for you,' declares the Lord, 'plans to prosper you and not to harm you, plans to give you hope and a future'" (Jeremiah 29:11). I was captivated by the realization that I was not only designed by God, but that He had a plan for my life.

Furthermore, I discovered that God says I am precious to Him and that He loves me!

> *Do not fear, for I have redeemed you; I have summoned you by name; you are mine... everyone who is called by my name, whom I created for my glory, whom I formed and made.*
>
> —Isaiah 43:1, 7

Me? Me! He has created *me* for *His* glory. I certainly had a difficult time wrapping my head around that one!

When I thought about my life and the mistakes I had made and recognized the sins I had committed, I realized that I didn't deserve God's grace. But God didn't see me—and doesn't see me—the way I saw myself. In fact, in Romans 5:8, Paul tells us, *"But God demonstrates his own love for us in this: While we were still sinners, Christ died for us."* While I was a sinner! Christ died for me when I was at my worst—not after I sought forgiveness. Again, I was humbled that He loved me that much!

I started to see myself through the eyes of God and tried to understand that when I put my identity in Him, I had no choice but to change my thinking about what I believed about myself. These scriptures challenged me to think differently and to recognize that I wasn't a mistake; I was loved and wanted.

As I processed these truths, I argued with God because I thought I knew myself better than He did. I dangled platitudes to Him like "That's stupid" or "Yeah right," as if my knowledge of myself was superior to His knowledge of me. As I began to understand truths of Scripture, and as I gained a deeper understanding of what my identity in Christ really meant, I confessed those disrespectful attitudes.

The Scriptures indicate that God wanted me so badly that He purchased me when He bore my sins on the cross. He actually paid for me with His precious blood and saved me by grace.

For you know that it was not with perishable things such as silver or gold that you were redeemed from the empty way of life handed down to you from your ancestors, but with the precious blood of Christ, a lamb without blemish or defect.

—1 Peter 1:18–19

For it is by grace you have been saved, through faith—and this is not from yourselves, it is the gift of God…

—Ephesians 2:8

I came to the realization that Jesus didn't endure death on a cross in order to purchase me and give me the gift of grace just so He could then toss me to the wind. Rather, because He paid for me with His precious blood, He placed incredible value on me, adopting me as His own.

For he chose us in him before the creation of the world to be holy and blameless in his sight. In love he predestined us for adoption to sonship through Jesus Christ, in accordance with his pleasure and will...

—Ephesians 1:4–5

Learning to put my identity in Christ was overwhelming, but it was exactly what I needed in order to identify myself with Christ as my Heavenly Father. This was opposed to the personal concepts I'd established myself on when I'd identified with my earthly father.

But knowing it in my head was one thing. Believing it in my heart would be quite another.

thirty-eight

About Louis

"Quick! Hide!"

His voice was adamant as he peered up from behind his bed. He motioned for me to join him on the floor, and then he quickly returned to his hiding spot. I acquiesced to his command and sat on the floor while I rested my back against his bed, staring at the beige wall just two feet in front of me. He returned to his knees and peered over the edge of his bed.

"The coast is clear," he whispered, assured that we were safe.

"Clear of what?"

He didn't answer. Rather, he took a deep breath. "Let's just sit here for a few minutes to be certain. No sense getting caught."

We sat together in silence, but I felt bewildered. This wasn't the father who had raised me—or was he? He had been diagnosed with a form of dementia which mimicked Alzheimer's and returned to the world he'd once known, the world he'd lived in prior to having a wife and family.

I had listened to his stories when I was a child. In an effort to legalize the sale of liquor, my father and grandparents had chummed with some pretty rough crowds.

Turning to look at my father, I remembered the story he'd once told about nearly drowning in the Detroit River after slipping off the dock while loading liquor onto a barge. Fortunately, someone in the darkness had noticed him and pulled him up and out of the water by the back of his shirt. Since then, he'd always had a fear of swimming.

In his early twenties, he had worked as a bouncer at Thomas's Inn. While dealing with the roughnecks, he'd helped monitor the flow of liquor through a garden hose which ran atop the ice of the river from Peche Island to the restaurant.

When my siblings and I were younger, my father told us many stories, including how my grandparents had smuggled liquor into the United States. According to my father, they'd filled old glass bottles with liquor, taped them to their bodies, then wrapped sheets around themselves to secure the bottles. Wearing extra large clothes over the sheets to hide their contraband, they'd cross the border to deliver the illegal liquids to their friends and families. Of course, they did this repeatedly without getting caught.

My recollections were suddenly interrupted when I noticed my father rub his head and look at his fingers.

"Am I bleeding?" he inquired.

I had learned to play along with his memories rather than challenge him.

"No," I replied simply.

"Good." He sighed, relieved that he hadn't been injured in his escape. "I'm glad the bottle was empty."

"What did he hit you with?"

"A wine bottle," he said matter-of-factly. "I've been hit before many times, you know!"

I was tired of sitting on the floor, but I was curious to know more. "Were you ever hurt?"

His response was automatic. "Sure! Even had to get stitches." As if a button had been pushed, he rose and sat in his chair. "How are you?"

I wondered whether he had just realized it was me in the room with him.

"Not bad," I responded, chuckling to myself.

But as the words left my mouth, I remembered a conversation my father and I had shared when he had first been diagnosed with Alzheimer's.

"I want you to remember something," he had said to me. "Even though today I remember that I'm forgetting, one day I will forget that I have forgotten. When that happens, I want you to not feel bad for your dear old dad because it will mean I am blissfully in a world of my own."

The purpose of my visit this day had been to confront him concerning the things he had done to me. I wanted to tell him exactly what I thought of him, as it was important for me to be able to place my anger where it rightfully belonged—on my earthly father.

But as I reflected on the re-enactment of his life's experience, I became very aware that he had entered his blissful world. He had become the little man who wasn't there, who wasn't there again today, and boy oh boy I wished he'd go away.

Unfortunately, we were both reliving memories. The difference was that he would soon forget his. How I wished I could forget mine. I hated the memories that haunted me, but I also craved for him to be burdened with the misery of the suffering I had endured.

After all, it was rightfully an affliction that he should bear. Not me.

See if there is any offensive way in me, and lead me in the way everlasting.

—Psalm 139:24

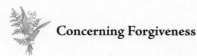 ### Concerning Forgiveness

What does it mean to forgive
The man who has sinned against me?
Does it mean to show my love
As I grant him sincere mercy?
Scriptures tell me to forgive
Just as Christ has forgiven me
But He gave mercy and grace
In order to set us free!

Forgiveness means to pardon
And to grant God His rightful place
To be Magistrate and Judge
Offering His mercy and His grace.
Forgiveness means I free myself
From falling into the grave sin
Of playing God. I free myself
From the pit I'm held hostage in.

For I am imprisoned by memories
And hurt, affliction and pain
Still enslaved by his heinous act.
What do I have to gain
By still holding this against him
Creating bitterness in my heart?
It's time to release him and let
My sovereign God play His part.

In forgiving I take control
(Where once I was so powerless)
By releasing him to God's hand
So God can disclose His vengeance.

Deeply I have felt the pain
And cannot deny it still exists
But with God's strength and power
I can now go on to freely live.

And if through this merciful act
God asks me to be gracious as well
Then not only will I serve him
But I'll love him and wish him well.

thirty-nine

Forgive My Father?

1995

ALMOST A YEAR HAD PASSED SINCE I'D TOLD MY PASTOR ABOUT MY childhood sexual abuse. He had listened, counselled, comforted, and without fail pointed me to Jesus and His love for me.

I had struggled with so many things: the triggers, Satan's lies, tears, and confusion. I had felt the pain. Deeply. I had wrestled with my sense of self-worth and started to appreciate the importance of placing my value and identity in Jesus Christ.

Now it was time to let go. I knew it was time. The problem was that I didn't know how to do it, and I wasn't even sure I wanted to.

Then it happened. My pastor sensitively challenged me to forgive my father.

Forgive my father?

Inside, anger burned, partly at my pastor, partly at my father, and partly at God. The "banty rooster" feathers in me stood on end and I thought I was going to explode!

How dare he challenge me? I thought. *Hasn't he heard me? Hasn't he heard all that I've been through? Hasn't he been listening to me?*

My pastor told me that when he'd had his devotions with the Lord that morning, he'd asked the Lord what he should speak to me about when we met. He believed that God had told him he should speak to me about forgiving my father.

While he explained to me how to forgive and gave me legitimate reasons to forgive, my thoughts focused on my prayer time that same morning. During my quiet time with the Lord, I believed that I'd heard Him tell me in no uncertain terms that I should forgive my father. It wasn't an audible voice, but an inner voice in my spirit: *"and after the earthquake a fire, but the Lord was not in the fire; and after the fire a still small voice"* (1 Kings 19:12, NKJV).

Although I sat in awe of the way God works, I felt trapped. Like a bird in a fowler's snare, I believed there was no way out, no other option but to be obedient to God's instruction. I knew that it was God and not my pastor who had directed me to forgive my father, but my emotions superseded my sense of reason.

"There's no way," I said. "There's absolutely no way I will forgive my father for that!"

Anger rose up in me. My stomach turned at the thought of being challenged with such a notion. Forgive? All I could think of was, *How dare he, how dare he! How dare He challenge me with this!*

The abuse was no longer in the dark, in its secret hiding place. The abuse had been exposed, but the pain was still in the depths of my heart. Although my pastor had been honourable in following God's instructions, the entire idea of forgiveness seemed preposterous, a completely silly notion to me. I held my ground. There was absolutely no way I would forgive him.

I reached for my purse so I could leave, but I politely waited when my pastor asked me to stay and hear him out. I listened to all of the biblical reasons why we should forgive, all of the logic as to why it's an important step, especially on the part of a Christian.

Next, he told me that I needed to *"[be] merciful, just as your Father is merciful"* (Luke 6:36). He quoted Hebrews 8:12: *"For I will forgive their wickedness and will remember their sins no more."*

But my inner voice yelled out, "But I'm not God! I can't forgive like God and I won't ever forget what he did to me!" Although I knew that my pastor had my best interests at heart and that he had been supportive, I still wanted to scream, "Don't you know what this has done to me? Haven't you been listening to me?!"

I wasn't angry at my pastor. I was just angry.

Concerned that anger would provoke an inappropriate and rude outburst, I decided to end the session. I was equipped with information and Scripture all about forgiveness.

But I was also armed with an incensed attitude and a heart which was unwilling to forgive.

Where can I go from your Spirit? Where can I flee from your presence?

—Psalm 139:7

In the same way, the Spirit helps us in our weakness. We do not know what we ought to pray for, but the Spirit himself intercedes for us through wordless groans.

—Romans 8:26

forty

Running, Hiding

Run. Hide. Running. Hiding. Always running, always hiding. Where can I run? Where can I hide? I wanted to run and I wanted to hide. I wanted to find a place where I would never be found. I wanted to disappear forever.

I drove several miles out of my way, then entered a small local provincial park. I travelled down lanes and dirt paths before finally tucking our teal-coloured van deep in the woods where I believed the thick branches created a place for me to hide.

I screamed at the top of my lungs and punched the steering wheel. My heart agonized over the pain still so deeply rooted inside me. My face was soaked with tears. Anguish tortured my soul. I wondered how long it would take for my heart to heal. I felt so emotionally broken.

Forgive my father? This went against everything I had ever believed about justice. I had done nothing wrong, yet I was supposed to forgive this man who had sexually abused me? It wasn't fair!

Anger joined me in my quest for justice and reminded me that I had every right to not forgive. Then anger goaded me to believe my reaction was justified.

He should be punished and should not be released of his responsibility, I thought.

Even the word forgiveness seemed like a misnomer. After all, the word "give" is stuck right in the middle, screaming at me and articulating an expectation that I had to give something to my father. Give him something? He didn't deserve anything. He especially didn't deserve to be forgiven.

I banged the steering wheel again with my fists and figuratively dug in my heels. I refused to forgive.

I knew that my pastor was still pointing me to Jesus and that he wanted me to be free from the pain and bitterness. He knew that forgiveness was the only way to truly let it all go.

"God wants us to pass on the marvellous grace that we have received from Him," I heard him say. "If we have truly been forgiven by God, we should forgive others."

But I was argumentative with God: "You can forgive! You're God. But there's no possibility for me to be like You."

I conjured up every kind of physical torture I figured he deserved. I started thinking in terms of *"eye for eye, and tooth for tooth"* (Matthew 5:38). After all, I had rights, and one of my rights was that I should be able to get even.

I remembered Ephesians 4:32: *"Be kind and compassionate to one another, forgiving each other, just as in Christ God forgave you."* My head told me that I needed to be kind to him, but my heart told me the opposite.

Anger rose up in me again. In my fury, I found myself growling like an animal. I pulled my hair, punched the steering wheel again, and kicked my feet, all in an effort to expel the emotions I felt. There was so much tension between my mind and my heart. I realized that this entire exercise of forgiving was not going to be easy.

As had happened earlier that day, I once again heard what I believed to be God's still small voice: *"Do not take revenge, my dear friends, but leave room for God's wrath, for it is written: 'It is mine to avenge; I will repay,' says the Lord"* (Romans 12:19).

I growled again, extremely frustrated. I needed to clear my head and get away. I needed to hide. While I ran my fingers through my hair and across the top of my head, I screamed again.

"Is there nowhere I can go to get away from you, God? Where can I go to hide from You?"

Psalm 139:7 came to mind: *"Where can I go from your Spirit? Where can I flee from your presence?"*

I felt trapped. I realized at that moment that I was unable to hide from God and unable to walk away from the responsibility that had been placed on me. I was being asked to give up my right to get even because one day God would settle the score. Then it became clear to me that God was asking me to let go of something which rightfully belonged to Him: revenge.

I knew that.

But.

The Lord said to Satan, "Where have you come from?"

Satan answered the Lord, "From roaming throughout the earth, going back and forth on it."

—Job 1:7

forty-one

Freedom of Forgiveness

I DECIDED THAT I WASN'T GOING TO FORGIVE MY FATHER. BUT BY doing so, I knew that it went against His command to forgive, and it was therefore an act of rebellion against God.

My disobedience opened a door for the enemy, Satan, who then tormented and attacked me with comments like "What kind of a Christian are you?" and "You can't even forgive your father!" At times he challenged me with statements that fed my own fleshly desires: "You don't need to forgive him. You're right! Look what he did to you!"

Darkness returned with a vengeance and reminded me of my unworthiness as a person and my insignificance as a Christian because of my aversion to forgiveness. Anger nourished my stubborn will, which began to drink from bitterness's well of contempt and resentment. Despair reminded me to hold fast to anger. This continuous loop caused me to lose hope and sink deeper into despair's arms of misery where I just wanted to give up and die.

The Holy Spirit had already told me to forgive, but my flesh wanted its own way. I agonized over the emotional battle that raged in me and created such a tension that it forced me into a crisis of my own will: my flesh vs. His Spirit that lived in me. In an attempt to balance the pros and cons of this turbulent storm, I painfully and intensely cried out to God—again and again and again and again.

"Why? Why? Why, Lord?" With no resolve to the question, I eventually found myself submitting. "Then please, Lord. Show me. Teach me."

I reflected on Christ's death on the cross and envisioned myself in His presence. When I looked at Him, I saw Him looking back at me. At that moment, I knew that He had compassion on me and that He desired to wrap His arms of love around me. Although I believed He was asking too much of me, I was aware that He wanted me to let go of the pain, and my right to it, so that I could be free of the anger, bitterness, and despair that heavily weighed me down.

He then spoke to me through His Word: "*Get rid of all bitterness, rage and anger, brawling and slander, along with every form of malice. Be kind and compassionate to one another, forgiving each other, just as in Christ God forgave you*" (Ephesians 4:31–32).

I already knew that I should forgive because Christ forgave me, but then I realized what it was that my pastor had been trying to say to me: I needed to forgive because it would free me from Satan's ability to take advantage of me.

And what I have forgiven—if there was anything to forgive—I have forgiven in the sight of Christ for your sake, in order that Satan might not outwit us. For we are not unaware of his schemes.
—2 Corinthians 2:10–11

I was faced with a choice that would determine how I would live the rest of my life: either I would live in the bitterness of unforgiveness or in the freedom of forgiveness. With that thought in mind, I considered that when Christ forgave me, He was both merciful and gracious. He showed me mercy by not punishing me for the wrongs I had done. He then asked me to follow His example: "*[be] merciful, just as your Father is merciful*" (Luke 6:36). Christ then went one step farther and was gracious to me by giving me something I didn't deserve: eternal life.

Based on Christ's model of forgiveness, I decided that I could be merciful to my father by not punishing him for the wrongs he had done to me. In addition, I would release my right to judge my father in exchange for my freedom to be released from that responsibility.

At the time, I wasn't in a position to give him anything beyond my mercy, but I hoped that one day my heart would be healed enough so that I would be able to love him, pray for him, and perhaps even serve him.

The Lord told me to forgive. I wanted to be obedient. But it was so hard.

After much soul-searching, I made a new decision. I asked my husband, our pastor, and the pastor's wife to surround me and prayerfully support me as I prayed. I told the Lord that with His help, I wanted Him to be my father's Judge. I no longer wanted to carry the pain from my childhood.

When I finished praying, the tears I had cried daily for eleven months stopped. A load of weight was lifted off of me. I felt so free!

The healing had begun.

forty-two

In the Hands of God

THE CHURCH YOUTH CHOSE THE BEAUTY AND SERENITY OF Northern Ontario for their canoe and portage trip. Just four weeks after I had prayed to forgive my father, I was packed and ready to help chaperone that active and energetic group.

I enjoyed the quiet, the beauty, and the magnificence of the oak, elm, and maple trees that stood tall and strong in this part of the world God had created. I appreciated the varieties of evergreen trees and inland lakes blackish-green in colour. In an awkward yet confident way, I claimed ownership of the world that weekend.

> ...for every animal of the forest is mine, and the cattle on a thousand hills. I know every bird in the mountains, and the creatures of the field are mine... for the world is mine, and all that is in it.
> —Psalm 50:10–12

While exploring the woods, the youth retrieved two fallen white birch tree trunks and tied them together in the shape of a cross. They then laid the cross on the ground near our campfire.

That evening, while everyone gathered around the warmth and light of the fire, our youth pastor invited everyone to write a message to Jesus on a blank cue card and nail the card onto the cross. On my card I wrote, "Thank You, Jesus, for being my Saviour, for dying for me, for taking my sins away, and for carrying all of my pain. I love You. Darlene."

Only the Lord knew the significance and depth of my message to Him.

Later that evening I heard my daughter exclaim, "Mom! Look at the cross!"

The moon was full and bright and reflected its light on the white cue cards, seemingly highlighting our messages to Jesus.

It occurred to me that the names nailed on that particular cross were just a small depiction of the love God demonstrated for mankind when He sent His son to die for the sins of the entire world. My card was just one small representation of the love Christ has for His children.

I left camp that weekend knowing in my heart that Jesus Christ loved me.

❦

Following the four-hour canoe and portage trek through Algonquin Park, we returned to our vehicles only to discover that a three-quart bag of milk had been left in the car for the entire weekend. The milk had fermented in the heat of the vehicle and the bags had exploded. The vehicle stunk to high heaven! It didn't take long for the sour odour to permeate our nostrils, clothes, and skin.

After travelling nine hours southwest through bumper-to-bumper traffic on a holiday weekend, we finally arrived back at the church.

I smelled horrible.

When I wasn't greeted with a happy and excited throng of people giving hugs and hellos, I just assumed it was because I stunk so terribly; it was quite understandable that no one dared approach me or the others who had been in our vehicle. But then a woman came up to me in the parking lot.

"You need to go right home," she said. "Jake is anxious to see you."

I sensed intensity in her voice. Although I had guessed that Jake missed me, I knew that he hadn't missed me quite that much! I called home from the church, my heart melting when I heard his sweet mellow voice.

"Hello!" he answered.

"Hey! We're home!"

Then I heard shakiness in his words: "You need to meet me at the nursing home as soon as possible. Your father's taken a turn for the worse and the doctor has asked that your family gather around."

Due to my most disgusting odour, I opted to first go home and clean up. A short while later, when we arrived at the nursing home, my father had already slipped into a coma.

He died the following evening, just one month after I had prayed to forgive him.

My heart broke. I had forgiven him based on mercy, not punishing him for the things he had done to me. I had hoped that one day my forgiveness could turn into grace, to someday sit by his side and feed him his dinner, to someday love him even though he couldn't seek repentance or reconcile with me.

But now I would never be given the opportunity to show him that grace, and as such I could only pray that the Lord would be both merciful and gracious to him.

Dear friends, let us love one another, for love comes from God. Everyone who loves has been born of God and knows God.
— 1 John 4:7

Four weeks earlier, my prayer had been that I could be merciful, and someday even gracious, to my father. My hope was that I could love him again. As 2 Corinthians 2:8 says, *"I urge you, therefore, to reaffirm your love for him."* But all hope of that someday ever coming was now lost. I felt cheated.

I anguished over my father's death and felt an intense pain from the loss of our relationship. But I also grieved because I didn't know whether he had made a commitment for Jesus Christ and whether I would see him again. I couldn't understand why God would ask me to forgive him only to then take him away. It felt so unfair.

My heart and body physically ached.

One day I shared these thoughts and feelings with my pastor, who declared, "Praise God!"

His response took me aback. "Praise God for what?"

"Although you will have to live with not knowing whether or not you will see your father again, be assured of one thing: you have forgiven your father because you can wish him well, and you wouldn't want any better for him than to have him sitting at the feet of Jesus!"

My desire to see him in heaven was certainly a form of wishing him well.

Do not repay evil with evil or insult with insult. On the contrary, repay evil with blessing, because to this you were called so that you may inherit a blessing.

—1 Peter 3:9

...do good to those who hate you, bless those who curse you, pray for those who mistreat you.

—Luke 6:27–28

I had forgiven him, but there were days when my feelings vacillated between forgiveness and contempt. This clouded the forgiveness I had extended.

My pastor had previously warned me that it would be necessary for me to repeat the process of forgiveness over and over again, that as long as the feelings of revenge returned I would need to forgive again and again, always relying on Christ's power to be able to do so. By doing this I ensured that judgment stayed in its proper place: in the hands of the Lord.

I learned that forgiveness is God's gift to me. Each time that despair, anger, and bitterness raised their ugly heads, I would pray a prayer of forgiveness again. This became yet another step towards my emotional and spiritual freedom.

forty-three

The China Doll

I TURNED FORTY LESS THAN TWO MONTHS AFTER MY FATHER DIED. I hadn't felt like celebrating.

By the time Christmas arrived, I wasn't doing well emotionally, possibly because grief had taken hold. I couldn't wait to get through the holiday season; it felt uncomfortable to feel so horrible yet have to put a smile on my face.

Immediately prior to Christmas, I attended a support group for women who had been sexually abused. The facilitator showed a video during which Dr. Richard Dobbins encouraged us to see ourselves transformed from old ragdolls to beautiful china dolls.

Without knowing that I'd watched that video, my three daughters gave me a beautiful china doll as a Christmas gift. There she was, so delicate and perfectly made. Her light brown hair, hanging in ringlets around her face, was adorned with a bow. She wore ivory-coloured pantaloons and a lace dress. Her face appeared to be hand-painted, and her green eyes and brown eyebrows resembled my own. Her soft body was made of cotton stiffly filled in order to support her head, arms, and legs, which were made out of china. She was absolutely gorgeous! She brought tears to my eyes. The sensitivity of my children warmed my heart.

But then something else extraordinary happened. One of my nieces brought me a Christmas gift. That in itself was unusual, as my nieces and nephews didn't make it a practice to purchase their aunts and uncles gifts for Christmas, so I really wondered what it was.

"Auntie Dar," my niece said to me as I started opening the gift, "do you remember when I was younger and I used to collect dolls? I collected all kinds of dolls, some old ones and some new ones."

"Well, yes, I do remember."

"Do you remember giving me your old doll, the one you used to play with as a child?"

"Yes," I replied. "I remember."

I remembered giving her my old doll, but I had long forgotten what the doll looked like.

She then motioned for me to finish opening the gift, and there in the wrapper was the doll I had used to play with as a little girl. Except, unlike the fragile china doll I had received from my daughters, this doll was really well-used. Her hair was matted, the clothes were dirty, and her moveable eyes were broken and rolled back into her head. Everyone around us chuckled, because she was a pretty sad-looking sight.

But I was struck by the underlying meaning of receiving those two dolls for Christmas—one old, from my childhood, and the other brand-new, from my adulthood. The one represented the old me, the one who had been abused and was worn out and whose hair was matted and whose eyes didn't quite see life clearly. The poor little doll even looked abused!

The new doll represented the new me, the new me who was beginning to understand her relationship with Christ and His love for her, including the love He even had for that abused child. It was as if the new china doll represented how Christ sees me—not abused, not confused and worn out, yet beautiful. It made me realize that in spite of my sins, fallacies, and weaknesses, and despite my brokenness, Christ sees me through His eyes, the eyes of the Creator. The new doll and all her beauty showed me what I might become when I allowed Christ to touch my life.

I wondered if I could ever be as beautiful as that China doll. Then I wondered, if I could picture myself as that China doll cradled in the tender open arms of Jesus, I too might care about myself in the way He cares for me.

I knew that Jesus hadn't abused me, hadn't stopped loving me, and hadn't stopped caring for me or about me. I knew that He had created me as His china doll, and as such He treasured and valued me. I also realized that Christ restores, and that He was restoring me from an old ragged doll into a beautiful China doll. One day, He would restore me and heal me.

The Doll You Hold
March 28, 1966, 12:30 p.m.
By Victoria Meadows

The doll you hold is just a doll so sweet
With a little of my love
You hold it in your tender hands
To treasure it with love complete
And as you love and care for it
With a cradle all its own
Just think of all the love you have
Where you have your own little home

I think of times when I too
Would hold and tend to it with care
I would never want to part with it
Til someone else would share
All the love I had for it
Making clothes and fuss and all
To fit its little body
That old rag like little doll

But if you keep on tending it
With kind and tender hands
You'll give it to your own my dear
As time does expand
Then you can say here is a doll
One of your very own so fine
And that dear old granny made
Just for you because you're mine

If I say, "Surely the darkness will hide me and the light become night around me," even the darkness will not be dark to you; the night will shine like the day, for darkness is as light to you.

—Psalm 139:11–12

Be alert and of sober mind. Your enemy the devil prowls around like a roaring lion looking for someone to devour.

—1 Peter 5:8

forty-four

Darkness, Anger, and Fear

I<small>T WAS COMPLICATED TO DEAL WITH MEMORIES FROM MY CHILDHOOD</small> at the same time that I grieved for my father. Once again I was overwhelmed with emotion. Somehow I managed to move through the steps of my life, but the negative thoughts and feelings I had about myself broke down my defences. Darkness had been an ever-present intruder in my mind, haunting me with dreary thoughts, including thoughts of suicide.

Anger and darkness teamed up against me as they broke down my spirit and convinced me to believe so many lies. I was so tired of wrestling with the negative thoughts. I was exhausted from trying to remain positive.

At times I was encouraged by the Scriptures, but rather than bask in the sunshine of those truths, I tarried with darkness, because it felt like darkness understood my sinister thoughts. Then darkness and anger enlisted fear, who was strong and mighty. Fear did not leave: he brought fear of evil and fear of the devil.

One day, I was home alone cleaning the house. As I dusted the television I clearly heard a loud voice bellow, "Why don't you go kill yourself?"

It was not a question. It was not a suggestion. Rather, it was an authoritative direction.

My hands shook and my knees buckled; I was forced to the floor. I knew that this wasn't my thought, and I believed with all of my being that I was in the presence of evil. I believed that it was the enemy, Satan himself, challenging me to give up and commit suicide.

I immediately repeated the verse: *"You, dear children, are from God and have overcome them, because the one who is in you is greater than the one who is in the world"* (1 John 4:4). The evil left. But only temporarily.

The attack continued, sometimes in my mind and sometimes physically. There were times when I felt an evil presence behind me or I saw a black shadow move beside me. On occasion, evil demons harassed me as they climbed on my back, taunted me, haunted me, and told me I was of no value. Again, as a defence against evil, I quoted Scripture.

Over time, darkness, fear, and anger wore me down, and that's when I entertained the thought of suicide. I rationalized the irrational and considered whether death was an option to living, especially to living with this ongoing assault on my mind.

My thoughts grew deeper and darker. Fear crept in, and I became afraid of my own self, afraid of what I might do. I also became afraid of Satan, his lies, and his forces of evil. I didn't mean to give Satan so much credit, because I also knew I was responsible for making decisions and entertaining the thoughts that pulled me down, but I believed that I wasn't only fighting a battle against depression; I was fighting a battle against darkness for my own life. In essence, I was fighting a spiritual battle.

Satan sent his soldiers to wreak havoc; they created such confusion and chaos in my mind that it became a life and death conflict. As John 8:44 says, *"he is a liar and the father of lies,"* therefore anything he told me was a lie. But I was unable to discern the difference between his lies, which he often disguised as truth, and the truth itself. This may have been because of what I already believed about myself.

I also failed to recognize that *"there is no truth in him [Satan]"* (John 8:44). I hadn't understood the truth of John 10:10, where Jesus explains the difference between Himself and Satan. In that verse, Jesus refers to Satan as the thief and to Himself as the giver of life: *"The thief comes only to steal and kill and destroy; I have come that they may have life, and have it to the full"* (John 10:10).

Jesus defeated Satan on the cross when He forgave our sins. But since Satan had (and has) continued to roam about on the face of the earth, He made (and makes) every effort to attack God's children. Unfortunately, partly due to my lack of knowledge of the Scriptures, and partly due to my lack of understanding the tactics of the enemy, I wasn't prepared for the battle.

The war raged so severely that I thought I had lost my mind. Although I believed that the thoughts of suicide weren't always my thoughts, they were present and persistent. I was aware that I lived in a sinful world and was exposed every day to things that are evil. But I also knew that I had, over the years, exposed myself to things that were not of God. As a result, I had given the enemy some wiggle room in my thinking, a place where he could hold things against me as if he was blackmailing me.

I compared this to a situation I had once found myself in while in seventh grade. On the last day of school, the principal had given out awards at our school assembly for perfect attendance. I had been very excited, and somewhat proud, because I had maintained a perfect attendance record in spite of moving to a new school that year and in spite of having had three different teachers.

But for whatever reason, when the awards were given out, my name was missed on the list of recipients. I was extremely upset. When I went home for lunch, my mother felt my disappointment and gave me permission to skip out of school that afternoon. Going one step further, she gave my older sister and me money to go to a show in the afternoon on the condition that I didn't tell my brothers.

But when my brother returned home from school he asked me, "Were you in school this afternoon? I didn't see you."

"Yup," I blatantly lied. "Sure was!"

"Liar!"

"Was too," I shouted back.

I knew I had lied, but I was in over my head. If I had told him I had skipped out, then I would have had to tell him that I had gone to the show. If I had told him I had gone to the show, I would have had to tell him that our mother had given me the money to go, and I would also have had to tell him that she had given me permission to skip out of school.

So I maintained the lie. "I was too in school!"

At that, my brother reached into his back pocket and took out a perfect attendance certificate with my name on it. Apparently the awards ceremony had continued in the afternoon and I had been invited to go onto the stage. But when I didn't go forward, because I wasn't in school, my brother went up onto the stage and received the award on my behalf. He'd even lied to the principal in front of the entire school, explaining that I had been sick that afternoon.

Although it had been a good cover-up on his part, and although he'd chosen to do it, it also meant that I had given him some power over me. In the end, he held this over me for the entire summer. Whenever we got into a disagreement, he would simply remind me, "I still have your perfect attendance certificate!" He sounded so smug, his eyes gleaming. And whenever he wanted something, like a cool drink, he would ask me to wait on him in that same superior tone, lording it over me. I had no choice but to do what he asked.

Certainly the current situation was much more intense than the one from seventh grade, but the idea was similar.

When I was a teenager, I had dabbled with the occult. I'd invited friends in our neighbourhood to join with me as we had séances around our dining room table and tried to connect with the dead. Satan had used that evil against me later by putting thoughts into my mind that were not of God. In addition, I experimented with a variety of other cultic practices; since these things were not of God, the enemy used them against me and reminded me of my unworthiness as a Christian because I had put one foot in his camp, so to speak.

Also, at different times of my life I had been exposed to the idea of suicide. On one occasion, when I was approximately eight years of age, I overheard my father and my mother talking about my father's best friend who had hung himself. I overheard every detail about the man's death, how my father had been forced to cut his friend down, and the agony he'd felt over that.

When I was in high school and my mother was drinking so heavily, I often thought of ways I could harm myself: I envisioned throwing myself down a flight of stairs in an attempt to get rid of the emotional pain I struggled with at that time. Then when I was eighteen years old, my cousin committed suicide. I will always recall the anguish and sorrow that my Uncle Phil expressed at my cousin's funeral.

Of course, my own sin also entered the picture: sins of rebellion (mostly against God), sins of pride, and even the sin of wrongful expressions of anger.

However, despite all those experiences, I knew that the words I heard while dusting the television that day—"Why don't you go kill yourself?"—weren't mine; they were the audible words of the enemy. Even though I knew this, I took ownership of the thought and claimed it as my own.

I made a decision: I wanted to die. I felt I could no longer live with the pain.

I took the irrational thought of suicide and I made it something very rational. The oddest part was that even though I knew the thought was irrational, I rationalized it and convinced myself that I wanted to die more than anything else in the whole world. I believed that my children and husband would be better off without me.

I believed the lies Satan told me, that I was unlovable and that if I committed suicide all my troubles would be gone.

I planned and I schemed. I made elaborate plans of how I would commit suicide so that it would look like I had just gone missing, to minimize the impact on my family. After all, I truly did love them. In fact, that was why I was going to get rid of myself, because in my mind I had decided that their lives would go on and that they wouldn't have to put up with me being depressed and crying all the time. My illogical thinking became logical, at least to me.

In addition, I decided that I would still go to live with Jesus because He had forgiven me and would forgive me for even that. So I asked the Lord to forgive me for my foolishness of heart and to please take care of my family. I asked Him to take me peacefully into His arms of love.

As I sank deeper into darkness's cloak of insignificance and obscurity, any sense of self-worth vanished, along with any care I had in the world.

I made a specific and detailed plan: to go to the barn and hang myself. One night, I waited until everyone was sound asleep, especially Jake. Then I climbed out of bed without making a sound and tiptoed to the doorway of our bedroom.

Suddenly, Jake sat straight up in bed and looked at me. I was thoroughly stunned, and somewhat angry. There was absolutely no reason why he should have awakened.

"Why are you awake?" I asked, ticked off with him.

His answer blew me away. "I don't know why I'm awake. I only knew that I had to wake up and tell you that I love you."

I felt caught, but also awed. I had no choice but to head back to bed. I lay there wide awake, struggling with spiritual forces: Satan, who wanted me dead, versus God, who wanted me alive. Like a teeter-totter landing hard each time it toppled, my head hurt from the vacillation. I felt unlovable yet was told I was loved. I couldn't comprehend the discord in my head and in my heart.

The conflict I struggled with was certainly in my thoughts, and specifically in what I believed about myself. I saw myself as absolutely nothing, and my deepest feelings about myself pointed continually to an individual who was garbage, useless and worthless. That's what the adversary, the father of lies, wanted me to believe. But God wanted me to believe the truth: that I was loved, worthwhile, and valuable.

I knew I had to change my thinking.

Do not conform to the pattern of this world, but be transformed by the renewing of your mind. Then you will be able to test and approve what God's will is—his good, pleasing and perfect will.
                                                                  —Romans 12:2

A war raged, a spiritual war in the heavenly realm and a war in my mind.

Many years later I heard a pastor explain, "There is no Switzerland in this war. You are in one army or the other. You can't have it both ways. From the moment you make a commitment to Jesus Christ, you are part of a war and therefore you are to be engaged in conflict. As such, we need to put the armour on: God does not put it on us. We need to remember that Jesus, *'having disarmed the power and authorities, he made a public spectacle of them, triumphing over them by the cross.'"*[6]

In an attempt to help me break free from the snares of the evil one, my own pastor pointed me to Jesus Christ and to scriptures that explained the spiritual world and spiritual forces. As I prayed for freedom, others prayed over me. I began to understand that I needed to know that Jesus was the Commander-in-Chief of the army and that He had triumphed over Satan and his angels by dying on the cross. My job was to understand that I needed to be continually prepared to do battle.

Submit yourselves, then, to God. Resist the devil, and he will flee from you. Come near to God and he will come near to you.

—James 4:7–8

...be filled with the Spirit...

—Ephesians 5:18

Be alert and of sober mind. Your enemy the devil prowls around like a roaring lion looking for someone to devour. Resist him, standing firm in the faith...

—1 Peter 5:8–9

[Understand that] no weapon forged against you will prevail, and you will refute every tongue that accuses you.

—Isaiah 54:17

Finally, be strong in the Lord and in his mighty power. Put on the full armor of God, so that you can take your stand against the devil's schemes. For our struggle is not against flesh and blood, but against the rulers, against the authorities, against the powers of this dark world and against the spiritual forces of evil in the heavenly realms... Stand firm then, with the belt of truth buckled around your waist, with the breastplate of righteousness in place, and with

---

6   Colossians 2:15.

your feet fitted with the readiness that comes from the gospel of peace. In addition to all this, take up the shield of faith, with which you can extinguish all the flaming arrows of the evil one.
—Ephesians 6:10–12, 14–16

I had already been a Christian for a long time, yet I hadn't learned that there was a battle for my life. It made me feel uncomfortable, because I didn't think I was that important, nor did I believe that my life was central to the Christian faith, or to Christ, to the point that spiritual beings, including Jesus Himself, would battle for me. Yet with my thoughts about my lack of significance, I knew I was battling for my life. It gave me consolation to know that Jesus was battling too.

As I grew in my understanding of this battle, I learned that I didn't have to do the fighting. I just needed to believe that Jesus had already fought the battle and that He had won the victory over Satan. As I grew to appreciate the work Jesus had done for me on the cross, I was also able to declare my rightful place in Him and declare Him as the Victor.

I knew that the darkness was spiritual and that my thinking was distorted. But I also considered whether there might have been a physiological explanation for the depression. As a result, I sought help from my family doctor, who prescribed an antidepressant. When she asked me whether I was having thoughts of suicide, my reply to her was short and simple: "Nope."

I lied. But I was so afraid that if I told her I'd had thoughts of suicide she would put me in the hospital. I well recalled visiting Aunt Victoria in the psych ward when I was young, and I didn't want to go there.

Over time, the antidepressant helped to readjust the chemical imbalance in my brain, which gave me some advantage as I continued to work through the grief and my childhood issues.

A couple of months later, I read a passage in Luke about a son who asked his father for an early inheritance. After his father gave it to him, the son left his father's farm, squandered his money, and partied until such time that he found himself penniless.

So he went and hired himself out to a citizen of that country, who sent him to his fields to feed pigs.

—Luke 15:15

I saw myself in that young man because I hadn't been willing to wait on the Lord or trust Him for my life. By wanting to end my life before its due time, I had been asking the Lord for my early inheritance.

I pictured Jesus looking at me, His eyes lovingly welcoming me to come closer to Him. That was when I saw the scars on His hands, the same scars that had been described to me by my Sunday school teacher when I was eight years old. In that split second, I knew that I wanted to live. I wanted to live for Christ and to live with Christ walking with me through this life on earth, no matter what. When I raised my head, my eyes met Jesus's eyes and I said, "I want to live."

At that moment, the load which had been on my shoulders lifted.

For several days, I told no one of my encounter. I crawled out of bed each morning and returned to bed each night with the same exclamation on my mind: "I want to live."

What, then, shall we say in response to this? If God is for us, who can be against us?

—Romans 8:31

Once again I felt hope and knew that I could rest in that hope because He had already overcome the evil of the world.

Freedom.

Uphold Me, Lord

What gain would there be
To end all pain and misery
By my own hand?

The gain would be mine
But for those left behind
The pain would start

So what's to be gained
By transferring the pain?
Nothing at all.

Surely God will prove
His awesome daily love
By sustaining me.

For you created my inmost being; you knit me together in my mother's womb. I praise you because I am fearfully and wonderfully made; your works are wonderful, I know that full well. My frame was not hidden from you when I was made in the secret place, when I was woven together in the depths of the earth. Your eyes saw my unformed body; all the days ordained for me were written in your book before one of them came to be.

—Psalm 139:13–16

forty-five

Two Steps Forward and Three Steps Back

1996

I HAD A PRECONCEIVED NOTION THAT A CHRISTIAN WASN'T EVER supposed to feel depressed, that a true Christian should lean on the strong and everlasting arms of Jesus. As such, I felt ashamed of myself, because my faith hadn't been strong enough.

To add insult to injury, I was then told by well-meaning Christians that I should "just take it to the cross and leave it there!" I wondered what that cliché even meant. But when I heard Christians mock other Christians because they suffered with depression, I felt irritated and disturbed. Without disclosing my own struggles, I attempted to speak up in favour of others only to have Bible verses rather passionately, and sometimes judgmentally, tossed back at me, like 1 Peter 5:7: "*Cast all your anxiety on him because he cares for you.*"

I understood the importance of trusting in Jesus as my Saviour to carry my pain and to lean on Him during those anxious times. But the abuse which had been inflicted upon me greatly affected my ability to trust. How was I able to totally trust a Heavenly Father when my earthly father had proven in so many ways to be untrustworthy? As a father, he had been irresponsible in protecting me as his child. He had abused me! As a father, he hadn't been dependable. Rather, he had allowed a drunk and obnoxious man into our home. As a father, he hadn't held himself accountable for the atrocities of his behaviour. He had laughed it off as if it meant nothing.

As I later discovered, learning to trust God as my Father took time. I worked hard at changing my faulty thinking, especially the ways in which I thought about myself. But there seemed to be no end to the emotional upheavals in my life. Each and every time I felt like I had made some emotional headway, circumstances out of my control set me back. I would hear my husband say, "It feels like you go two steps forward and three steps back."

This was the case when, approximately six months following my father's death, a seemingly normal sun-rising, alarm-blaring, arms-stretching morning turned out to be a most unordinary day. I received a telephone call at work from my cousin who had drifted in and out of my life. She and I had been close for a short period of time when we were teens. We had been born the same year, so when our families had gotten together, on those rare occasions when we did, she and I had paired up and hung around together. Our goals in life had been very different; she had wanted a husband and a family; I had wanted an education. Ironically, we ended up having children around the same time.

I was glad to hear from her, but the nature of her call, especially given my struggle with depression, opened a new wound for me. That telephone call will always stand out in my mind.

Since she called me at work, I answered the phone in my usual professional tone, and then quickly shifted to a more relaxed manner once I realized that it was a personal call. Following our usual "Hello" and "How are you?" my cousin went on to tell me that her mother, Aunt Eleanor, was dying. She'd had an aneurism. Aunt Eleanor and I hadn't been close, but I had respected her, the mother of nine children and full of energy. She had always spoken her mind and said it exactly the way she saw it; I always knew where I stood with her. I had admired that about her and always wished I could be more like that.

As the phone call continued, it occurred to me that my cousin had picked up some traits from her mother.

After telling me that the doctors couldn't do anything to help my aunt, my cousin went on to say that her mother wanted me to know the truth about my life before she died. My cousin stated this matter-of-factly.

I gave my head a double-shake, because that seemed like a rather strange thing to say.

What truth could someone know about me? I thought. *Since I'm the one living my life, shouldn't I be the only one to know the truth about myself?*

"There's no easy way to tell you this," my cousin continued brusquely. "The lady who raised you, the lady I called Auntie Anne, was not your real mother. But it's okay." She continued in an effort to be reassuring. "We'll always be cousins!"

As I tried to take in the impact of this news, I remained quiet. I didn't respond. I was stunned. I was shocked. Our conversation had been very brief, and when I realized that it was over I robotically said, "Thanks for calling!"

As I hung up, I burst into tears. Needless to say, I felt blindsided.

My emotions were still raw from my father's death and darkness still hovered over me, leaving me in a vulnerable state. I felt somewhat defenceless against any negativity that came into my life, never mind something of this magnitude.

I reeled, trying to process this information. I immediately projected all kinds of theories about who my real mother could be. Since my father had remarried just a year following my mother's death, I automatically suspected that my stepmother might be my biological mother.

I decided to call her.

"Are you my mother?" I asked as soon as she answered the phone.

Not knowing the background to my question, she began to laugh hysterically.

"No," she replied through laughter in her heavy French accent. "When would I 'ave 'ad time to 'ave 'ad an affair with your father, what with six kids of my own, let alone 'ave another child with him? *No.* I am not your mother."

It would have been so much easier for her to reassure me, to say something like "Don't be silly, of course Anne was your mother."

Instead she continued with that dreaded word—but.

"But," she continued, "I don't know much about it. I do know that your father 'as some pictures 'ere which 'e kept in an encyclopaedia. I 'ad wanted to put them out in the living room wit' the other pictures, but 'e wouldn't let me as 'e told me that they were pictures of 'Darlene's mother.'"

Although perplexed, I was also intrigued. "Go on."

"Well, I 'ave seen pictures of your mother—of Anne, that is—when she was younger. The woman in this picture is for certain not a picture of Anne. I 'ave no idea who this woman is."

At that, she suggested that I go to her home and she would give me the pictures.

A short time later, she greeted me at the door, her short hair neatly coiffed and curled, as usual. The short blond curls framed her petite face; she had few wrinkles and certainly didn't appear to be a woman in her early eighties.

While standing in her kitchen doorway, I towered over her. She was likely even shorter than my mother had been—at least now, the woman who I thought my mother had been!

"'i!" she said, welcoming me. "'ow are you?"

"Very confused and upset," I replied. I told her more about my conversation with my cousin earlier that day.

My stepmother then handed me a picture which immediately absorbed my attention. She told me that she had previously seen two more pictures, including one of a woman alone, but she had been unable to find them.

I looked intently at the old black and white photograph. In it, a man and woman in their late forties or early fifties sat with a younger woman on a loveseat in the foreground; two other young women stood behind them. The younger women all appeared to be in their twenties and each was beautifully but modestly dressed.

The gentleman was wearing a black suit and the older woman a print dress which ended mid-calf when she was sitting; the top of the dress was blouse-like, with buttons up to the neck and short sleeves. Her white belt matched her white laced-up oxford shoes, which had been very fashionable in the 1940s. The young woman sitting beside her wore white peephole pumps, which were also common to that era.

The young women's dresses all had three-quarter to full-length sleeves. Each of the dresses ended just below the knee and were all slightly formfitting while accentuating their petite figures. The younger women looked similar but they didn't appear similar enough to be sisters.

I didn't recognize anyone in the picture.

All four women in the picture had similar hairdos: curled, cut above the shoulder, and pulled back off their faces. Although all of them wore lipstick, the younger women each appeared to wear a deeper colour and a heavier coat than did the older woman.

The picture appeared to have been posed, and it may have been taken at a professional photographer's studio. There was a window and a curtain in the background as well as a short staircase banister which seemed to be part of a backdrop rather than an actual railing. The flooring in the picture had a distinct pattern of squiggles and stars; it was difficult to tell if it was carpet or linoleum.

I felt numb as I stared at the picture in my hand, looking at the faces, the eyes, and the women's other physical features, trying desperately to discover anything recognizable, knowing that one of these women might be my biological mother. My head spun. My heart whirled. I felt so confused.

When I later showed the picture to each of my siblings, they didn't recognize anyone either, and as a result the picture became a mystery. I floundered in the unknown and wondered how I would get to the truth.

I decided to visit my two aunts, Isabel and Eleanor, as well as a friend of my parents, in the hopes that they would reveal the women's identities. My pastor's wife offered to go with me.

We started first by visiting my mother's best friend. After explaining the nature of our visit, she intently looked at the picture and pointed to one of the young women, identifying her as Martha Meadows. Amazingly, when we later met with my aunts, they said the same thing and explained that Martha had been Aunt Victoria's sister-in-law; both Victoria and Martha had married into the Meadows family. Unfortunately, Victoria had died a few years earlier and Martha's whereabouts was unknown. The identity of the remaining women in the picture remained a mystery.

I asked a lot of questions but didn't get any more answers. I left these visits with the distinct impression that my aunts and my mother's friend had been sworn to keep a deep dark secret.

As the years passed, I tried to uncover the truth about my mother and my birth and was determined not to leave a stone uncovered. Every time I was presented with a clue, no matter how small, I exhausted all theories and possibilities in the hopes of uncovering additional clues.

One day I went to the hospital to get some medical tests done. Since there was a lengthy wait between the tests, I ventured down to the Department of Health Records to obtain a copy of my birth records. After making my request in the basement office, the kind young lady behind the counter immediately told me that this wasn't something she could do right away. I calmly stated that I would wait. Since I wasn't going anywhere, I patiently sat in the waiting room and read magazines.

I must have been a sad-looking sight—no makeup, hair dishevelled, wearing just two Johnny shirts (one backwards and one forward) and a pair of thin hospital slippers. It's possible that the Director of Health Records took pity on me, because I hadn't waited long before she called me into her office. She told me that there was no record of my mother giving birth to me. I told her that my mother had always told me that I was actually born on October 2 and that my father had written the date down wrong on my birth certificate. She then also checked that date but was still unable to produce a record of Anne giving birth to a child then.

As a result of that meeting, I ordered a long-form copy of my birth certificate, which showed Anne and Louis as my parents.

I remained perplexed in the face of this seemingly contradictory information. If indeed the hospital had no record of me being born to Anne, then how was it that there was a long-form birth certificate which showed me being born at that hospital to Anne?

It was a mystery.

ॐ

I had progressed over the years in understanding that my value and identity as a person lay in who Jesus Christ said I was, not in the things that had happened to me. However, this information about my birth negated the work I had previously done. Darkness sometimes returned and challenged my sense of self-worth, reminding me that in addition to being unloved and abused, I had also been discarded.

My gloomy feelings returned when I couldn't find answers. At those times, it became necessary for me to pause my search for the truth. I would set everything aside long enough for me to recharge my emotional battery. This became a means of self-preservation. Then, once I had recuperated enough, I would resume the search. This resulted in a very slow progression towards the truth.

Three years passed from the ominous telephone call from my cousin. I decided that it was once again time to visit my aunts. In particular, I decided to beg my Aunt Isabel for the truth.

During our visit, Aunt Isabel told me that shortly after I was born there had been a family get-together at which time I was passed around. When someone asked who the baby belonged to, the family was simply told that I was Anne's. Everyone in the family knew that Anne hadn't been pregnant, but rather than ask any further questions they just accepted the story.

"Darlene," Aunt Isabel explained in her British accent, "you need to remember that it was the mid-1950s, and in those days people didn't ask questions. We were quite aware that your father had had indiscretions prior to that, but rather than bring those suspicions to the forefront, people just kept quiet."

When I challenged her, pointing out that it was no longer the 1950s, that I was forty-three years old, and that people had been given ample time to tell me the truth, she further justified the family's choice to remain quiet.

"You must know that we knew your dad had been unfaithful to Anne before," she continued, choosing her words very carefully. "It happened at least once that we knew of, so there was reason for us to believe he had been unfaithful again. Although we were all aware that you might have been another one of *his* children, we simply didn't ask any questions."

Aunt Isabel's face looked both worried and frightened; her voice cracked when she spoke, and I noticed that her bottom lip quivered. I was convinced that she knew the truth, all of it, and that she wasn't telling me.

I begged her to retrieve her old photo albums so that we could find a picture of my mother, Anne, pregnant with me. She gave me a sympathetic look and said, emphatically, "No."

After I had approached the request from several different angles, she finally leaned forward and caught my attention

"There aren't any pictures, Darlene."

I felt that she knew more than what she was telling me, so I pressed the conversation further. I was determined not to leave her home that day without an answer.

Finally, she broke down, with tears in her eyes.

"Maybe... maybe you are Victoria's child."

I was stunned. Her statement certainly caught me off-guard.

Maybe? I thought. *What in the world does that mean? Victoria's child? Weirdo Aunt Victoria?*

I couldn't believe my ears! In an effort to distract myself, in an attempt to ease the pain of that possibility, I focused on a bottle of vitamins sitting on her kitchen table. Even the remotest possibility of Aunt Victoria being my mother made me tremble.

When I left Aunt Isabel's house that day, I again called my Aunt Eleanor and pressed her for more information. Her abrupt response angered me.

"Listen," she said. "Why don't you call your cousin, Robert? He knows a whole lot more about the Meadows family tree than I do!" But then she softened, acknowledging my concern. "I believe Robert has the answers you are looking for."

I felt like she was just dispensing with me, and I also felt violated. After all, she was the one who had started this whole I-gotta-tell-you-the-truth-before-I-die stuff! Nevertheless, despite my apprehension over having to turn over another stone, I made the call.

Robert was my first cousin and the oldest of Aunt Victoria's children. He had two younger brothers, William and David. Robert and William had been the sons of Aunt Victoria and her first husband, Uncle Bill. It had been my understanding that when Victoria and Bill separated, the boys stayed with their father due to Aunt Victoria's inability to properly care for them. In spite of that, Uncle Bill had always made certain that both Robert and William spent time with our family. I had fond memories of hanging out with them when I was younger. However, because Robert was nine years older than me we weren't close, and as such we had lost track of each other over the years. Nevertheless, he was open to meeting with me and we made arrangements to get together.

I was so excited, anticipating that he might finally be able to shed some light on the truth of the identity of my biological mother. Hopefully he could explain to me who the women were in the picture my stepmother had given me.

But on the day Robert and I had planned on meeting, Robert's brother William called me.

"Are you sitting down?" he asked.

"No," I replied. "But I can if you think I should."

While holding the telephone to my ear, I awkwardly reached behind me for a kitchen chair and sat down. I sensed hesitation on William's part. His voice shook as he continued.

"Robert died of a massive heart attack this morning."

Apparently Robert had experienced chest pain while driving to work, so he'd driven himself to the hospital where he'd died in the parking lot. He had been just fifty-three years of age.

I was in shock. I felt the loss of a cousin, but I also felt the loss of the truth of my identity. Had the secrets about my birth died along with him? It felt like a piece of me went to the grave that day, and I began to resign myself to living with not knowing.

Two weeks before my forty-fourth birthday, I packed everything away—the picture, the notes, and the little information I had gathered from newspapers about my father. I put it all away in a box, intending to forget about it and move on.

But every so often I would dig out the picture and run my fingers over the figures of the young women and see the details of their eyes, hands, faces, and the shapes of their heads in an effort to determine if there was something, anything, that might seem familiar.

I always came up empty-handed, broken-hearted.

Nine years later, Aunt Isabel passed away too, at which time I had the opportunity to talk briefly with my cousin William.

"Any idea where David is?" I asked at the funeral, peering into William's dark brown eyes. I also took in his tall, lean frame and salt-and-pepper hair, evidence of a man who had hit midlife.

David was the only cousin I'd been unable to connect with who might have some information regarding my biological mother. Although David had a different father from William and Robert, and thus wasn't connected to the Meadows family tree, they still shared the same mother. I had not given up on hope.

"I drive by David's place once in a while," I said. "But I don't know whether he and Doreen would be open to me stopping in."

I was reminded of the many times I'd had opportunities over the years to meet up with David and Doreen. A few years after Jake and I had married, I'd been doing some visitations, representing our community's Welcome Wagon. David and Doreen had moved into the area, and I had visited their new home, approximately five minutes from my own house. Our children attended the same school. On occasion when Jake and I saw David and Doreen at the school, we shared hugs and had a short visit with each other. However, our conversations were limited to those times.

Whether or not it was the best decision, I had cut myself off from extended family because I felt the need to protect my own children. After all, to my best recollection, bad things happened when people drank. I didn't know whether David and Doreen drank, or how much; I only knew that I had to safeguard my children.

I also needed to safeguard myself—from the memories and from the triggers.

When I realized that my thoughts had wandered, I returned my attention to my conversation with William.

"Last I heard, David and Doreen had separated and David moved to Alberta," he said.

My optimism deflated. I made efforts over the next four years to find David in Alberta, using the internet to locate telephone numbers and addresses, but to no avail. Occasionally I would drive by Doreen's house in the hopes of dropping in to talk to her, but I was unsure how she would receive me. Preserving myself from the possibility of further rejection, I always changed my mind and drove by.

Eventually I gave up on my quest for the truth. I packed the pictures, notes, and documents away again and tried to forget about it, telling myself, *Who knows if it's true anyway?*

forty-six

Reconnected

November 2012

DARKNESS HAD DISSIPATED AND THERE WAS A NEW LIGHTNESS TO MY life. I had found new ways to cope and had held onto the fact that Jesus Christ was my Father. My bond with the Lord had deepened and I found daily comfort in my relationship with Him.

I continued to vacillate between whether I should try to find my mother or just forget about it. Meanwhile, living had taken over. My days and weeks were filled with the excitements of parties, graduations, youth events, and weddings as well as studying to finally finish my own graduate degree.

One day, I decided to thoroughly sort through some stacks of papers I had tossed into a box over the years. It was a perfect day for this meaningless task, which matched the mood of the November skies—dreary and grey, bringing with them the impending threat of winter.

While tossing some papers and keeping others, I came across an Avon brochure that had been put in our mailbox by Doreen many years earlier. I had kept it with the thought that I might one day need David and Doreen's unlisted telephone number, which was written on the back.

My immediate reaction was to dial the number.

I felt awkward placing the telephone call. Feelings of shame dangled in the air as I chastised myself; I should have been more responsible and loving over the years, checking in on my cousin, showing concern for him and his family's well-being rather than only connecting now in order to find out some information: David's whereabouts.

Nevertheless, I dialled the telephone number and left a message.

When Doreen called back, she seemed to immediately warm up to me. When I asked if she would tell me whether David was around—meaning, in the area—she simply replied, "Well, he'll be home from work in a little bit. Do you want me to have him call you?"

I was shocked. Then I shared with her that William had told me that they had separated and that David had moved to Alberta. Doreen reassured me that was not the case; in fact, he had lived in that house all along.

When David returned my call, I told him that I had some family history materials to share with him and wondered whether we could get together. Since he was very receptive to the idea, I gathered my notes, pictures, and documents, including the picture of "Martha" with the unknown family and headed over to his house that very evening.

While Doreen, their son Edward, and his fiancée Kate sat together with us in the living room, David and I reminisced about our lives and the times we remembered being together when we were children. He shared about his life with his mother and his brothers.

That time of sharing between David and I was enjoyable and entertaining. I had the pleasure of sharing stories with David and his family about things my siblings and I had discovered about our mothers' parents, our grandparents.

But this time of sharing was also emotionally heavy at times. David told me that the last time he'd lived with my family, he'd come home from school one day to find his things sitting in boxes and bags in the front hall of our house. According to David, my mother had told him he could no longer stay with us and then introduced him to a worker from Children's Aid. He told me that no explanation was offered. He didn't know what he had done wrong. He didn't even know whether he would see his mother again. He was then asked to help carry his things outside, at which time he and the lady headed out the door. To add to an already perplexing situation, David told me that when he turned around to say goodbye to his Auntie Anne, my mother, the last thing she said to him was, "I refuse to raise another one of Victoria's children."

David hadn't only felt bewildered by this statement, but also sad because he hadn't been given a chance to say goodbye to me.

I was flabbergasted by this entire scenario! He had only been nine years old at the time, and I was absolutely horrified that my mother had done this to him. It also went against my parents' philosophy that there was always enough food to go around.

I struggled with being unable to comprehend why my mother had done this to a little boy, let alone her nephew. By that point in my life, I was aware that my mother's relationship with Victoria had been strained at times and that Victoria had often used Anne to get her own way. I could only imagine that perhaps my mother might have felt that Victoria had used her again. Maybe she had thought it was time for her to put her foot down. Maybe David had just gotten caught between my mother's frustrations and Victoria's seemingly irresponsibility.

On the other hand, I was also aware that my mother had tried to do her best for David. After all, he had stayed with us through his birthday and through the Christmas holiday. She had also managed to ensure that he received a present for Christmas.

I wish I knew whether she had struggled with her decision to call Children's Aid. I tried to give my mother the benefit of the doubt, but it was difficult at times because I agonized over what David must have felt. I admitted to myself that I was very confused, and my speculation wasn't helpful. Besides which, the entire point had become moot; nothing could change what had already happened.

More important was my perplexity regarding my mother's comment to David that she refused to raise another one of Victoria's children. It seemed like an odd thing to say, but given Aunt Isabel's insinuation that Victoria might be my mother, it made me wonder. Was this another clue that needed to be pursued?

I shared with David and Doreen about my quest to find my biological mother, and I showed them the picture I had been looking at for so many years. The picture was passed around the room and both David and Doreen took time to look at it. But it was Doreen who seemed to study it most intently. Suddenly, she left the room and returned a few minutes later with a couple of pictures from Victoria's wedding to her first husband, Uncle Bill.

One of the black and white pictures showed Aunt Victoria, Uncle Bill, my mother Anne, and an unknown gentleman standing together. My grandmother stood off to the side, holding the railing of a banister to a staircase. Both Aunt Victoria and Anne wore dresses which stopped just below the knee, with full skirts, three-quarter-length sleeves and high collarless necklines. Aunt Victoria was wearing a dark-coloured tam which leaned over onto one side of her head. A long black and white feather adorned the other side of the tam. Both my mother and grandmother wore rich flower corsages. The four adults in the bridal party were smiling, but my grandmother wore a black dress and looked very stern.

This picture appeared to have been taken in the same photographer's studio as the picture I had received from my stepmother. It had the exact same flooring as well as the same backdrop, window, and curtains. Although it still didn't explain who Martha Meadows was and how or if I was connected to her, it suddenly made sense that the picture would include Martha, since it had been taken at Victoria and Bill's wedding. My picture seemed to at least have a context now, even though we didn't know who the individuals in it were.

The five of us looked at each other curiously yet knowingly. Our mouths hung open, our jaws dropping in disbelief as we wondered what truth lay hidden behind the photographs of that wedding night. We sat quietly for a while, as if in shock, and pondered.

I felt closer than ever to solving a mystery that had eluded me for years.

"If I didn't know better, I would think that you and I were brother and sister," I said to David as I packed up my things to head home. "The good Lord knows, and He will continue to direct us to the truth."

David's eyes widened. "We believe that way too."

We hugged each other and bade our good nights.

forty-seven

God's Timing Is Perfect

DAVID LATER TOLD ME THAT AFTER I LEFT HIS HOME THAT NIGHT, there was a flurry of discussion and comments. He too thought we might be brother and sister. Over the years, Doreen had often said that she thought I looked like his mother. That night, Doreen told David that it wouldn't surprise her at all if I turned out to be his sister.

David's son Edward and his fiancée Kate participated in the discussion. They shared how fascinated they were to learn the things they had about our extended family. These were stories they were hearing for the first time, things they hadn't known because David hadn't known.

David told me that he knew some things about my family because he had spent time with us. But that was the first time he had heard anything about his grandparents. In fact, it was the first time he had even heard their names. He attributed this to the fact that he had grown up in foster care. But it was interesting that even though David didn't know much about our grandparents, it was he and Doreen who'd had a picture of our grandmother I had never seen.

After our get-together that night, David was convinced the mystery was close to being solved.

"I think we cracked the case," he told his family.

David knew that the only way to get to the bottom of this would be to have our DNA tested. He even told Doreen that he would gladly pay half. And once he had made up his mind about something, there was no stopping him from moving forward.

But they both thought the entire situation was rather odd. After all, I had gone to their house in anticipation of gathering information about the Meadows family tree, only to leave with possible information about my own roots. As they further discussed this as a family, Doreen encouraged David to pursue the answers he needed.

"God makes no mistakes," she said to him. "His timing is perfect."

There is a time for everything, and a season for every activity under the heavens...

—Ecclesiastes 3:1

forty-eight

DNA Testing

THE VERY NEXT DAY, DAVID CALLED ME AND PROPOSED THAT WE DO DNA testing. I was overwhelmed by that suggestion, as I hadn't thought of it. In addition, I needed time to consider the possible repercussions of such a test. If the DNA test showed that David and I were half-siblings, it would mean that my other siblings and I were also only half-siblings. Furthermore, I would have to admit that Anne hadn't been my biological mother.

Over the years, one of the strategies I used in order to keep darkness at bay was to maximize positive activities and resources in my life at the same time as minimizing stress. Since it was just a few weeks before Christmas, I felt that for my sake it was important to wait until after the holiday before moving ahead with the DNA testing.

Over the next several weeks, I talked to Jake and my children about the possible outcomes. Overall, they encouraged me to move ahead with it. I decided to call David back following the Christmas holidays in order to put a plan in place to have DNA testing completed.

But.

One evening in the early part of January, Doreen called to tell me that David was in the hospital. They had been out for supper one evening when David had told Doreen that he felt the food didn't taste right. Since he thought he had food poisoning, he went to the hospital. After conducting several tests, the doctor diagnosed him with cancer. He was hospitalized and then booked for major surgery; his prognosis was not good.

David was diagnosed with colon cancer and had developed a duodenal fistula, which allowed faeces to back up into his stomach. The cancer had spread to his liver and to several lymph nodes. He underwent an eleven-hour surgery to remove the cancer and to complete a resection of his colon. He was a very sick man.

While he convalesced at home, we spent time getting to know each other and catching up on our lives. David shared with me how difficult it had been leaving our home when he was a little boy because he hadn't known what he'd done wrong, and he'd always wished that I could have been with him. He shared with me that going into foster care had been frightening. He had felt scared and alone when he went into the homes of strangers. Not only had he not known the people, but he hadn't thought they really cared about him.

When he'd arrived at his first foster home, he had carried his own bags into the house and been introduced to the foster mother. She had shown him to his bedroom and told him to unpack his things while she went out to talk with the Children's Aid worker.

His foster mother had seemed nice enough, but his foster father had been very strict. There were a lot of rules which he had to follow. This was quite different from living with his mother, who had let him do pretty much anything he wanted and given him independence from a young age. He also wasn't used to routine and having a time for everything and an order to everything he did. However, he had been a compliant child, for the most part, which helped him make the transition to a foster home easier.

When his foster father arrived home from work, he took David to his bedroom and placed an extremely large colourful sucker wrapped in cellophane on the top of David's dresser. David had never seen a sucker so big or so colourful! His foster father told him that he needed to prove that he was an obedient little boy, and therefore he wasn't allowed to touch the sucker. He told David that he would come back to his bedroom at the end of each day to see whether or not he had eaten it.

This routine went on for several days until one day after school David finally succumbed to the temptation; the longing to eat that sucker just got the better of him. So he opened it and savoured every bite! But later that evening, when his foster father came into his bedroom and saw that the sucker had been eaten, David found out what a "good whipping" was, something his friend at school had once talked about. The next day, he was moved out of the home, having been deemed a child who couldn't be trusted.

I felt sad for David. I tried to process the unfairness of what his foster father had done to him. Deep down, I seethed with anger when I realized that he wouldn't have gone through that if he hadn't been sent away in the first place.

I also wondered whether things would have been different or easier for him if I had been sent away with him.

At the beginning of April, David decided he was strong enough to arrange for DNA testing to be completed.

Doing the DNA test was actually quite simple. The lab sent us several large Q-tips and our job was to simply swab the inside of our cheeks, then mail the samples back to the lab. David sat on one end of the couch in his living room, and I sat on the other end. Edward was our witness, for legal reasons, and he joined in the merriment while he watched his father and his father's cousin laugh and giggle as they distended their cheeks in unusual shapes while swabbing with the overgrown Q-tips.

David and I were both excited to get to the bottom of the truth about our lives. But as we swabbed our cheeks, we caught each other's eye when we realized that we had each created a rhythm with the movement of the Q-tips. Almost simultaneously, we broke out into song: "Huh. Huh. Who's your daddy?" Of course, this was followed by laughter on both our parts. Edward just shook his head as he joined in the fun.

Little did we know that we would discover, as time passed, many strange commonalities with each other.

forty-nine

A Final Goodbye

May 2013

I SUPPOSE ANY DAY'S A GOOD DAY TO FIND OUT THE TRUTH ABOUT oneself! I had anticipated that a written report from the lab would come in the mail at any time, but I hadn't expected that I would receive an official telephone call.

On my way home from work, I realized that I was near the graveyard where my mother and father were buried. Since there was no traffic behind me, I had the opportunity to be spontaneous; I slowed down and took the turn into the cemetery. While pulling up to the gates, I felt overwhelmed by a strange feeling. For whatever reason, making this stop on this particular day felt therapeutic.

I hadn't visited the graveyard in a long time, as I really did believe that my parents were no longer there; their bodies lay decaying while their souls lived on. I found the burial plot easily enough. When we'd left the cemetery on the day we buried my mother, I had counted the trees from her burial plot back to the cemetery office. Twelve trees in all. It had become ritual since then to count the trees which led to their plot. Of course, the trees were much taller now than they'd been more than thirty years earlier. A lifetime, really. But here I was, like a little girl, counting the trees again.

I stood looking down at the gravestone marker. I had seen it many times before, but today the little message on the corner of the marker caught my eye.

"Together forever!"

I laughed out loud, then looked around to see if anyone was around. After all, it might have seemed disrespectful to some to laugh in a cemetery. *Really?* I thought to myself. *Really. Let's think about this one.*

At the risk of being judgmental, I wondered whether my parents truly were together forever. After all, he hadn't been true to her even while they'd lived on earth, at least not in the biblical sense. He had wronged her in so many ways. He had been with so many other women. Him saying "til death do us part" seemed like a mockery of marriage.

I stood there for several minutes thinking about my parents and the life I'd had with them. I had to admit that even though we'd had a lot of rough patches, it hadn't been all bad. Did I think that they had loved me? I had to admit that I did. I also acknowledged that they had been my parents and that there must have been a reason that God chose me to be part of their family, whether I belonged to them biologically or not.

My thoughts took me back to a time when darkness had ruled my life, to a time when I had tried so hard to deal with the memories from my childhood. In an effort to get rid of the pain, I had written my father an angry letter telling him how much he had wronged me and the impact it had had on me. There, in the graveyard, in this exact spot, I'd sat on the ground in front of his grave and read my letter to him in a flood of tears. I had yelled and screamed at his grave that day, oblivious as to whether anyone else was around. My spirit had been so broken and my pain so deep. Then I had removed the vase which was supposed to hold flowers, ripped up my letter, and placed the pieces inside it. I then lit the pieces on fire and watched as the smoke dissipated into the atmosphere, symbolically burning the pain away while relieving anger's hold on me. I had prayed that my memories could somehow vanish that easily.

Hoping that this visit would represent another rung on my ladder towards emotional freedom, I looked again at the headstone marker.

"Goodbye!" I said.

On that day, it seemed like the right thing to do. It wasn't a goodbye in terms of saying "so long" or "until next time." There seemed to be finality to it. It was a once-and-for-all goodbye. A last stop. A marker on my road of life, so to speak.

It was strange. A little eerie, actually. I knew that my parents weren't there, so I wondered to myself, *Why am I talking to the dead?*

Perhaps it was the setting. After all, I was in a graveyard. But the mysterious part of it was how strongly compelled I'd been to say goodbye.

I left the cemetery feeling good, not ecstatic or euphoric, just calm.

Back on the highway, after travelling for just a few minutes, I decided to call home. After chatting for a minute, Jake matter-of-factly said, "The lab called."

He explained that although a written report had been mailed, the lab had wanted to give me a verbal report of the test results because they'd known I was anxious to find out, especially given David's failing health.

An uneasy feeling came over me. Even though I knew we had submitted the DNA swabs, and even though I'd known the test results would be coming, hearing that the results were in made my insides shake with anticipation and dread.

Jake sounded calm yet anxious to tell me the test results.

"And…?" I asked.

"Are you sitting down?"

He must have forgotten that I was actually driving. It was the laugh I needed to break the nervous tension I felt building in me.

"Of course I'm sitting down. I'm driving!"

"Well…"

ॐ

After talking to Jake, I immediately called David. He didn't answer the phone at home. My hand shook as I pressed buttons on my cell phone in an attempt to then try David's cell.

Finally, he answered!

"It's Darlene!" I mustered, oblivious in my angst that he likely had already known it was me from his call display.

He greeted me with his simple yet loving reply: "Hi there!"

"Hi back!" I said, hoping that I sounded more cheery than anxious. "Just wondering if you guys were going to be home later this evening?"

"Yup. Should be home in about an hour. We are just running errands. What's up?"

"Just need to talk about something." My reply probably seemed a bit cryptic.

"No problem. I'll text you when we get home."

While I waited to hear from David, I stopped to purchase groceries in order to pass the time. As I put items in my grocery cart, I couldn't concentrate. My mind was somewhere else—specifically, on my previous conversation with my husband.

While Jake had prepared to give me the news, I had thought about how sweet he was. Despite this bizarre situation, he had never wavered in his friendship and love for me. He had always encouraged and supported me. So many times I had wondered why he stuck by me, as I was certain that the drama in my family was too far out of his realm of understanding. I had worried about the stress this put on him and on our relationship. But he had seemed to take it all in stride.

Like so many times before, I praised God that He had given me such a man—a solid character of love and faith, a man who was devoted to me no matter what!

"You can call the lab back if you have any questions," Jake had said, "but they wanted you to know that you and David are half-siblings."

I attempted to process the news.

I didn't know it was possible to have so many emotions at one time running through my veins, to my heart, to my head, all attempting to be processed at the same time and competing for attention. They bounced off each other, trying to make sense of themselves. I'd heard the expression "mixed emotions" before, but this seemed to take the cake.

Finally, David texted and I headed to his house. When I shared the results of the DNA test with David, Doreen, and Edward, everyone began to cry. David grabbed me and held onto me—tight. He was so much taller than me that I was literally standing on the tips of my shoes.

"I have a sister," he cried. "I have a sister!"

"I have a sister-in-law! I have a sister-in-law!" Doreen exclaimed.

I was excited too, but I felt numb. I felt glued together. I couldn't go there.

I could not feel.
I would not feel.
Not there.
Not then.

∂❧

So you wake up one day and basically everything you believed about who you were and where you belonged has changed.

David was so happy, so excited. He had a sister and his children had first cousins. Doreen had a sister-in-law. I was happy about those things too. I had another brother and a sister-in-law and even more nieces and a nephew. These were all wins for him, and they were wins for me as well. But it also meant so many other things to me. I also felt like I had losses.

Anne was no longer my mother.

Victoria was now my mother.

Both women had died when I was in my twenties. I knew Anne, but I didn't really know Victoria. Although David had been in the care of the Children's Aid Society as a child, he had still somewhat known his mother. Our mother. I hadn't.

In addition, men who I had once believed to have been my cousins were now my brothers, one of whom had already passed away thirteen years earlier.

Anne had given birth to other children whom I'd grown up with. We were a sibling group of five. But now, we were only half-siblings.

My father, Louis, was still my father. I was unable to express, even to myself, my emotions regarding that!

My sense of belonging had been shaken.

∂❧

I was happy because I finally had the truth, but the test results changed everything.

Why had no one told me? I was fifty-seven years old and just found this out! While processing this new understanding of who I was, I realized this was the best-kept family secret I had ever known.

The anger welled up. Aunt Isabel had intimated that Victoria was my mother, but the way she had posed it, it had sounded as if she really didn't know for sure.

Then there had been the disappointments and lies which had accumulated over the years.

In the commotion and excitement, I looked at David and said, "I don't even know her birthday."

"October 17!"

His reply seemed almost robotic to my ears. It wasn't that I actually wanted specific information. It was more of a lament, a comment perhaps—a response to the mixed emotions I was feeling. Even though Anne had been gone for many years, I had always remembered her on her birthday: January 2.

I realized that I knew nothing about my own mother, my own flesh and blood.

But the truth had been exposed.

I received interesting responses from my siblings when I shared with them the news that Aunt Victoria was really my mother. But when I showed my sister Annette the picture of our grandmother at Aunt Victoria's wedding and how she looked so grim and serious, Annette told me that she had seen that picture before. In fact, she had a copy of it. When I told her that David had given it to me, I also asked where her copy had come from.

"I found it at Dad's one day," she said. "When he was getting ready to move, there were some old encyclopaedias tossed onto the floor. Three pictures slipped out from in between the pages. I took the one from Aunt Victoria and Uncle Bill's wedding, as well as a picture of Aunt Victoria. But I left the other picture because I didn't know who the people were."

At that, Annette showed me the picture she had of Aunt Victoria.

Annette had taken the other pictures my stepmother hadn't been able to find that day all those years ago. My sister had had them all along. Everything fell into place.

If I rise on the wings of the dawn, if I settle on the far side of the sea, even there your hand will guide me, your right hand will hold me fast.

—Psalm 139:9–10

For I am the Lord your God who takes hold of your right hand and says to you, Do not fear; I will help you.

—Isaiah 41:13

fifty

Who's Your Daddy?

MANY YEARS PRIOR TO RECEIVING CONFIRMATION THAT I HAD BEEN born to a different mother, I had started a practice which brought me great comfort. Whenever I felt low, I reached out my hand and asked Jesus to place His hand in mine while I quietly whispered, "Do you love me, Jesus?"

His answer was always the same, each and every time: "Yes, Darlene, I love you."

Softly I heard His voice. It never changed. It was always reassuring and always comforting.

Reaching for the hand of Jesus had become a comforting habit for me.

Shortly after I received confirmation that Victoria was my biological mother, it struck me that my father, Louis, must have had sexual relations with Victoria and that he had done so while he was still married to Anne. I was disappointed in my father.

My feelings grew raw as one of my favourite childhood memories of being with my father turned into repulsion. When I had been a little girl, my father and I had walked hand and hand to get groceries. I could still hear my mother, Anne, say, "Why don't you take Darlene with you?" She usually said it in a tone of voice that seemed to imply, "Get her out of my hair for a while." But I was okay with that, because it meant I could walk down the sidewalk with my daddy and hold his hand. I always felt so proud that he was my father and that I was his little girl. Even though I had struggled with some painful memories of him over the years, that one gentle memory had often brought me comfort. It was the one last good memory I had of him.

But the realization that he had impregnated Victoria took away that sense of pride and comfort. I was now irritated by the consequences of his actions and the years he'd spent building lies upon lies. I was angry that he hadn't told me the truth about the identity of my biological mother. I also resented the ongoing pain I'd had to deal with in life because of this man, because of this man I had called Dad.

As I tried to fall asleep, these thoughts repeated themselves over and over. I wished I could find a way to somehow press the delete button and discard them, discard everything into a trash box somewhere.

I started to cry, but I muffled my sadness in my pillow so as not to wake Jake, who lay sound asleep beside me. I didn't want to be my daddy's little girl, nor did I want to inherit the mess he had left for me.

I eventually fell asleep. But some time later, I had a dream. In it, I was walking down the sidewalk, that same sidewalk I'd peered out to when I was hiding under the porch, that same sidewalk where I'd ridden my tricycle, that same sidewalk I'd walked down when I was a little girl and held my daddy's hand. But in the dream, although I tightly held onto a man's hand, I looked up to discover that I wasn't holding my father's hand; rather, I was holding onto the hand of Jesus as He had reached down His hand to hold mine.

"Thank You, Jesus, for being my daddy," I said, crying. I repeated it over and over. "Thank You, Jesus, for being my daddy." It must have been the sound of my voice that awakened me, for I recall saying it out loud. "Thank You, Jesus, for being my daddy! Thank You, Jesus, for being my daddy!"

What would I do without Jesus?

One of the treasures David had of our mother's was her poetry. One day, he brought the poems to me.

"She's written about you!" David said. "You'll see all the poems about 'Darling.'"

That was mind-boggling, but I was also amazed by the commonalities in our writing and how some of the themes in her writing were so closely related to mine, even though our poems had been written more than thirty years apart.

Walk With Me

O, Lord,
This morning take my hand in Yours
Lead me along the way
Walk beside me where'er I go
Please don't let me stray
Keep me safe in your mighty arms
Where I always will be
Comforted and protected
When others hurt me
For loneliness cannot prevail
Nor sadness fill my soul
When my Saviour walks so near
This daily will be my goal.

Darlene's Thirteenth Birthday
October 2, 1968
By Victoria Meadows

I'm talking I'm walking
Through this world of sin and woe
If you're unhappy and burdened
He'll give you peace from woe

I'm happy with Jesus
He's the best friend in the land
For I'm walking with Jesus
And He's the one who holds my hand!

My frame was not hidden from you when I was made in the secret place, when I was woven together in the depths of the earth. Your eyes saw my unformed body; all the days ordained for me were written in your book before one of them came to be.

—Psalm 139:15–16

 **Comforted**

Heavenly Father who watches over me
Preserving my fragile life
In accordance with Your word
Effortlessly sweeping
Your precious plan on me

Christ Jesus who died for me
Adopting me as your own
In accordance with Your laws
Lovingly lavishing
Your saving grace on me

Holy Spirit who washes me
Bonding me in Christ's blood
In accordance with your love
Continually giving
Your comforting self to me

fifty-one

Victoria, My Mother

By the time the truth about my life was fully uncovered, all the family members from my parents' generation had passed away. As a result, there was no one available to explain Victoria's relationship to my father or whether that was the reason for the demise of her marriage to Uncle Bill. But in our discussions, David and I gathered enough details to develop two possible scenarios.

It was both possible and probable that Victoria had had an affair with Louis. If that were the case, Uncle Bill's heart would have been broken once he found out. It was common knowledge that Bill adored Victoria and the fact that she had been with the younger and debonair Louis would have been a double betrayal. Furthermore, Bill would have known that his own much older, scrawny, and somewhat emaciated physique couldn't compete with Louis's tall, sturdy, and very good-looking frame.

Victoria's relationship to Louis may have started years earlier, since she, like Anne, had worked at the same nursing home where Louis's parents had resided. She too would have noticed Louis when he came to visit his parents. Given Louis's engaging personality, he could have flirted with Victoria. She might have interpreted this as Louis leading her on and might have become confused when Louis started dating Anne instead of her. Based on Victoria's consistent jealousy of Anne from the time they were little, it's also possible that Victoria found it hard to accept that

Louis chose to date Anne instead of her. As a result, Victoria's envy of Anne might have lingered long past her own marriage to Bill.

This is all based on speculation, of course, but it's certainly in the realm of possibility.

The facts have already been established that Louis left Anne when he dashed off to Florida. But I've always wondered whether Victoria felt bad for her sister, who was left behind broken-hearted. Or was Victoria's heart also broken when she found out that Louis had actually taken off with her own sister-in-law, Martha Meadows? Was that the woman he had run away with?

Given the era and the hurt Louis had caused Anne and her family, Victoria should have known that Louis was used goods and not a positive influence. And given the disconnect between Anne and the rest of her family following Louis's return to Canada, Victoria should have known that her family wouldn't approve of any relationship with Louis. It certainly made me wonder, *What was she thinking? What kind of charm did he exude?* Once the affair started, I wonder whether she felt like a shame-faced serpent sneaking around behind her sister's back.

Taking into account the date of my birth, Victoria's affair with Louis must have started no later than two years after Louis returned from Florida and reconciled with Anne. This made me wonder how long the affair lasted and how long it went on before it felt comfortable. My thoughts turned sarcastic when I pictured the two of them together. Did they feel like they were meant to be together, destined somehow by fate? I also suspect that my father didn't learn from his former affair, and as a result he had no regret or guilt over doing it again.

Sometimes I wish I could have been a little mouse in the corner in order to satisfy my curiosity as to whether Louis whispered sweet nothings in Victoria's ear, or told her that he loved her, or that she was his all. I also wonder whether those were the words that rang out in her mind when she found out that she was pregnant with his child. I could just imagine his reaction when he heard the news that she was pregnant: "You're what!?"

Perhaps my own insignificance is coming to the surface here, but given that I grew up with his attitude that children were a curse, I presume that he was greatly irritated by this. I picture him as he paces back and forth across the kitchen floor, rhythmically rubbing his chin with his thumb and fingers as he mutters to himself, wondering what he should tell Anne—and if so, how.

Did he feel remorseful for what he had done—for what he had done again? Did he consider running away like before, or did he face the situation like a man and take responsibility for his actions and for the child? Is it possible that Victoria announced her pregnancy and was silent regarding the identity of the father? In that regard, it's therefore possible that Anne never knew Louis was the father. After all, it would have been one thing to raise your sister's child and another thing altogether to raise your sister's child knowing that your husband was the child's father!

In one of Victoria's poems she wrote, "I had built a garden of roses around my heart, a garland of roses—a sweet lover's knot that only he could have. I believed his promises, that they were entwined with truth and built out of love. And now, our sweet lovers' knot was broken." Had she given her heart to Louis? Was it Louis who broke it?

So was it an affair that brought them together? And was the baby conceived in love?

The second scenario contains two strong possibilities. Since I was born in the early part of October, the likelihood is that I was conceived on New Year's Eve. Perhaps Louis and Victoria didn't have an affair, but rather a one-night stand, a quick moment of pleasure. Either way, this moment would have been approximately two years and four months after he returned from Florida. I find that thought to be disturbing.

The other possibility is that Louis had a quick moment of pleasure at Victoria's expense. If that were the case, that might provide some explanation for the night when Victoria thought Louis was going to kill her with a hammer. Consequently, what others perceived to be her delusions and hallucinations may have been actual fears based on former traumatic experiences and events.

Amongst her poetry, Victoria wrote this on a slip of paper: "Anne: love. Louis: hate"

There may be no significance at all to this note. Then again, maybe there is. You decide.

Was it an affair? A one-night stand?

Or was it a sexual assault?

During our childhood suppertime tales, my parents told the story that on the day I was born, they were provided with a police escort to the hospital because my father had been speeding. As a child, I always assumed that it was because my mother, Anne, was in labour with me.

When I started to put together the pieces of my life and delved into the details of this story, I came to the conclusion that I had been misled. In fact, my parents didn't even own a car at the time I was born. As I uncovered more details regarding my birth, it became apparent that their story was a huge cover-up to disguise the truth about my birth.

When I considered Victoria's diagnosis of paranoid schizophrenia, the medications she might have taken, and the fact that Uncle Bill had been granted custody of their two older sons, it's most likely that my father was granted custody of me. Or she may have given me up and willingly granted custody to her sister and her husband.

That thought is supported by another poem I found in Victoria's journal:

Take her away, she is yours, if you will
Take her away, she is yours, if you will
To some other land perhaps, cure her ill
As soon as I could, I made haste for the shore.
I replenished my strength and supplies galore
And I helped the fair maiden her health to restore
Once on our way with fresh air and sun
I saw some red colour in my pretty one.
Then she spoke o so softly, "I loved him so."
My sister betrothed him so I wanted to go.

I was lost on the desert 'til you came by.
God bless you, I'll love you until the day I die!

If indeed that poem is reflective of the day I was born, I can only imagine how difficult it must have been for Victoria. Had she heard the announcement that the baby was a girl? Did she see the doctor as he handed her baby over?

When I interpret the rest of the poem, I wonder whether she was sedated. I wonder whether she was delusional or in deep emotional pain. When I consider that the poem may have been written about me, I feel comforted by the last line that she loved me.

I wonder whether there were times when she felt like her heart had been ripped out of her chest and whether the turmoil she felt was too much to bear. Given the events of my life, I am convinced there were many times when she wanted to tell me, when she wanted me to know that she was my mother. But her sister and brother-in-law wouldn't consent, and as a result the truth remained a secret.

Take her away, she is yours, if you will…
God bless you, I'll love you until the day I die!

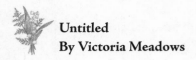

Untitled
By Victoria Meadows

I could forget you, little darling
If you'd stay away from me
Although you know I love you
I don't want you to go from me

But I can't keep you, you know
You belong to someone else although
I love you dear and always will
I could forget if you'd stay away from me

fifty-two

Adopted by Christ

ONE JUNE DAY WHILE I TRAVELLED ALONG THE COUNTRY ROADS, MY mood was one of ease and delight. The winter wheat danced in the gentle breeze, its golden hue highlighted by the mid-afternoon sun. The adjoining fields of soybeans and corn were still green and distinct, yet they added colour, texture, and beauty.

Nestled between two fields of green, I entered the driveway which led to the foster home. As I parked the car near the house, nine-year-old Amelia greeted me at the car door.

"Trixie had her puppies!" she excitedly declared.

"She did?"

"Yup." Then, without skipping a beat, "Four! Come see!"

Amelia grabbed me by the hand and led me towards the porch of the old farmhouse where four beautiful golden retriever puppies busied themselves nursing. The mother lay relaxed, seemingly unaffected by our presence.

But I suddenly became aware of a most unusual sight: the nursing mother was not the golden retriever I had previously met, Trixie. Instead, the mother nursing the puppies was a black and brown German shepherd.

"I'm a little confused," I said to Amelia. "Where's Trixie?"

"Oh, that's Sheba!" Amelia pointed to the German shepherd. "Trixie got sick right after her puppies were born and she couldn't take care of them. So my foster dad, Mr. Martin, got an idea. On that very day he had seen that our neighbour, Mr. McIlroy, put a sign at the road which said 'Free puppies.' I heard my foster dad on the phone tell Mr. McIlroy that

Trixie got sick and couldn't feed her puppies." Amelia lowered her voice in an attempt to sound like her foster father: "Yup. Yup. Might work! Okay then. See you in a few!" Her voice then returned to normal as she continued her story. "Next thing I knew, Mr. McIlroy showed up here with Sheba. He told her to lie down and she did! Then my foster dad brought Trixie's puppies one by one and laid them down on top of Sheba."

I listened intently as Amelia gave me the play-by-play of how the puppies had started to drink from Sheba and how Sheba had lain there and let the puppies have their fill. Apparently Sheba had just weaned her six little puppies and so it was a perfect time for her to continue nursing Trixie's newborns. Amazingly, the golden retriever pups thrived and Sheba was given the credit for saving Trixie's young.

The purpose of my visit to see Amelia that day was to once again explain to her why she was living in a foster home. As I pet the beautiful puppies, I realized that Sheba's ability to care for Trixie's puppies was the perfect illustration for my next comment.

"I guess that makes them foster puppies," I said.

From the look on Amelia's face, I saw that she finally understood what it meant to be in foster care.

"Just like me!"

"That's right. Just like you! Since your mommy can't take care of you right now, you live with Mr. and Mrs. Martin. Even though they aren't your real mom and dad, they do everything your mom would do: they take care of you, feed you, clothe you, and love you. Just like Sheba's doing for Trixie's puppies. Except, of course, she isn't putting clothes on them!"

Amelia laughed as she patted Sheba on the head. "Thanks, Sheba. Good job, girl!"

As I looked back on Amelia's new appreciation of what it meant to be fostered, and as I recalled how Sheba cared for another dog's puppies, I was grateful for the example she set for Amelia on that day. But I was also grateful for the example she set for me because I realized that my mother, Anne, had not just fostered me in hopes that I would return to my biological mother once she got better. Rather, she had gone one step further and raised me as her own. Her obligation to me had been a life-long commitment.

If my mother, in her humanity, did that for me, how much more has Jesus done for me? I thought to myself. Since Jesus was sinless, the shedding of His blood made Him the perfect and final sacrifice to take away the sins of the world and to purchase me.

Look, the Lamb of God, who takes away the sin of the world!
—John 1:29

...the blood of Jesus, his Son, purifies us from all sin.
—1 John 1:7

For you know that it was not with perishable things such as silver or gold that you were redeemed from the empty way of life handed down to you from your ancestors, but with the precious blood of Christ, a lamb without blemish or defect.
—1 Peter 1:18–19

He redeemed me and then, when I decided to ask Him to forgive me for my sins, He made me His child.

For those who are led by the Spirit of God are the children of God.
—Romans 8:14

As is typical for God, after being merciful and gracious to us He once again went even one step further. He didn't just foster me; rather, He adopted me as His daughter and David as His son. He adopted us as His children.

For you did not receive a spirit of slavery to fall back into fear, but you have received a spirit of adoption. When we cry, "Abba! Father!" it is that very Spirit bearing witness with our spirit that we are children of God...
—Romans 8:15–16, NRSV

Then, as His children, He made us His heirs!

So in Christ Jesus you are all children of God through faith... If you belong to Christ, then you are Abraham's seed, and heirs according to the promise.

—Galatians 3:26, 29

So you are no longer a slave, but God's child; and since you are his child, God has made you also an heir.

—Galatians 4:7

As His heir, everything He has belongs to me.

Now if we are children, then we are heirs—heirs of God and co-heirs with Christ, if indeed we share in his sufferings in order that we may also share in his glory.

—Romans 8:17

When I was little, I was incessantly teased on the schoolyard. Not because I was stupid or ugly, but because of the family I came from. Unbeknownst to me, I carried my father's reputation with me wherever I went, and as a result I suffered by being bullied and teased.

As I considered my relationship with Jesus as my Father, I realized that because I am connected to Jesus and put my identity in Him, because He is my Father and I am His child, I too carry my Father's reputation with me wherever I go. As a result, I too face sufferings, not only because I live in a sinful world but because "*everyone who wants to live a godly life in Christ Jesus will be persecuted*" (2 Timothy 3:12). With that new understanding, I understood that I needed to go through suffering in order to truly appreciate the healing I would eventually experience.

David and I shared tremendous joy because we had found each other. We rejoiced, because we had received proof that we shared the same genetic components in our DNA, enough to be able to call ourselves half-brother and sister, because we shared the same mother.

David and I also rejoiced because we had each put our faith in Jesus Christ and as such had become God's children. As God's children, we were spiritually brother and sister because we shared the same DNA through the shed blood of Jesus, our Heavenly Father.

I rejoiced because Christ suffered on my behalf. Because His self-sacrifice was an act of love for me, I will one day share in His glory when I am reunited with Him in heaven for eternity.

It astounds me to think that I did absolutely nothing to receive God's mercy and grace, yet over and above all of that He has adopted me as His child and made me His heir.

It made me wonder, *Who? Who does that?*

But God isn't any *who*. He is God.

fifty-three

His Plan for Our Lives

WHEN DAVID AND DOREEN LEFT THE ONCOLOGIST'S OFFICE, THEY were thrilled by the doctor's report. In some ways, David wasn't surprised that it was good news because so many people had been praying for him. He was looking forward to having more time to do things with Doreen. She had always been such a blessing to him. They were very well-suited to each other, being spontaneous and loving to just pick up and go.

"Pack a bag!" David would tell Doreen as set out for another of their adventures. "Dress for warm weather." Or: "Dress for the north."

David told me that he thought this spontaneity came from living in foster care and never knowing whether or when he would be moved. To cope with always feeling unsettled, he had learned to see the move to a new foster home as an adventure rather than something negative.

Doreen's kindness and compassion were exactly what David needed, especially given the childhood he had endured. Doreen loved David unconditionally and, like in most marriages, she extended forgiveness to him on many occasions. While living with cancer, Doreen had been David's tower of strength.

David was also looking forward to spending more time with his children. As young adults, they were all busy with their own families but certainly they still needed to have a father around, and in particular one who would support them and stand strong on their behalf.

Because he had been a young father, it meant he was also a young grandfather. David utilized his mix of spunk and spontaneity to create fun times and build memories for his grandchildren. On one occasion, when the two oldest grandchildren were having a sleepover, David woke them up in the middle of the night. He dragged them out of bed and whispered, "C'mon, let's go. Grandpa needs to eat a fudgesicle!"

They drove forty-five minutes one way to a twenty-four-hour grocery store where they purchased twelve boxes of fudgesicles and then ate them in the middle of the night! David hoped that his grandchildren would always cherish that adventure.

David was also looking forward to spending time with me, catching up and bonding as siblings—shopping, eating, laughing, and even crying together. Like me, David had a strong will and deep determination innately embedded in his character. That fortitude propelled him to keep going.

Although the cancer had shaken David, it had also strengthened his faith. He shared with me that he had gone forward in church and asked for prayer. People had prayed for him and laid hands on him.

"I have good news!" he said to me on the phone after his doctor's visit. "The doctor told me that the new drug is having an impact on the cancer. He says that my bloodwork numbers have dropped drastically, which is an indication that if things continue at this rate, I may have a couple of years."

"Praise the Lord!" I said, a predictable and encouraging response. "We will keep praying."

Cancer. An ugly thing!

Life changed quickly. David was up one day and down the next. My emotions yo-yoed too, tossed in one direction only to be suddenly tugged back on their own axis. That was the case for me when it came to receiving David's unpleasant medical news.

But David always just said, "It is what it is."

Since there was nothing he could do about it, he figured there was no sense getting upset. "It is what it is." He seemed so calm.

"The CAT scan showed that the cancer has spread and travelled to my lungs," he'd told me one day. "What's more, my liver is completely covered with tumours."

I wasn't calm. Instead, I felt an uneasy and tumultuous feeling in my stomach.

ೋ

Over the next couple of months, David and I spent time together. We talked, we shared, and on many occasions we cried together because of the experiences we'd had as children, and because we felt that we had missed out on sharing our lives together. We laughed together as we discovered the many characteristics we had in common, and we noticed that we were both very stubborn, sometimes to a fault.

We also realized that we had the same taste in foods. We both detested pork and beans and loved butterscotch!

One day, David asked Doreen to please get him some Mini-Wheats. As she headed to the kitchen, he shouted out to her, "I would like fifteen, please."

"What? Fifteen?!" Doreen had replied, astonished at such a specific request. "Who counts their Mini-Wheats anyway?"

When I started to giggle, David turned and looked at me quizzically. Amused and a little embarrassed, I quickly responded. "I do!"

The absurdity of this commonality between us caused everyone to laugh light-heartedly.

Any time after that, when we came across common interests or experiences, someone would verbally toss out, "It's okay. They both count their Mini-Wheats too!" And that would consistently send us and anyone else in the room into uproarious laughter.

As David and I grew closer, we shared some of the deeper struggles of our lives. Although there were certain aspects of my life I would have rather forgotten, I knew that I could trust sharing my heart's concerns with him.

We also battled together over many of the why questions. Why had God brought us together now, rather than when we were children? Why had God waited until David was battling cancer? Although I recognized God's sovereignty, and knew that He makes no arbitrary decisions, I struggled with these questions. At these times, I tapped into my bank of memorized verses and was comforted by Jeremiah 29:11: *"'For I know the plans I have for you,' declares the Lord, 'plans to prosper you and not to harm you, plans to give you hope and a future.'"*

"His plan for our lives is perfect, David," I said. He just shrugged his shoulders. "I don't know the answers, but I believe we can never doubt God's plan for us, especially when we remember that He loves us."

Sometimes Doreen joined the conversation and encouraged both David and I to remember that God's plan and timing is perfect. She would quote Ecclesiastes 3:1: *"There is a time for everything, and a season for every activity under the heavens..."*

Both David and I would nod in agreement.

We spent time gathering pictures and documentation. Although the DNA test results clearly showed that we were half-siblings, they didn't say whether we shared a common mother or a common father. We came to the conclusion that we shared the same mother, based on the stories we'd been told. But I struggled with wanting to see some tangible evidence, perhaps in our mother's own handwriting. As a result, Doreen and David dug through boxes and papers, trying to locate anything that would satisfy the longing of my heart in this regard.

When they found David's baby book, Doreen immediately called me. "Hey chickee!" she said. "I found David's baby book. Victoria has written some very interesting information in that book. Why don't you come over?"

The three of us sat around their dining room table and opened that small, thin baby book. Worn in places with brown stains from possible water damage, the book detailed David's birthdate, weight, when he had walked, his first words, and other various facts, all of which were recorded in Victoria's handwriting. It was interesting to notice dates when he'd had the mumps and the German measles, as they coincided with the times I remembered also being sick with those childhood illnesses. Although we had been raised in two separate homes, it seemed apparent that we had spent time together when we were little.

We also noted that Victoria had written the name of David's biological father: Joseph Jones. I was quite emotional about this.

"Last night, I had specifically prayed that something could be found," I said. "Something in Victoria's own writing that would give more solid proof that she was my mother."

God answers prayer.

fifty-four

Clues from the Past

SINCE VICTORIA HAD IDENTIFIED JOSEPH JONES AS DAVID'S FATHER, that meant it couldn't have been Louis. The only way David and I could be half-siblings was by us sharing a common mother. The information Victoria had provided in that baby book was an answer to my prayers. It was the clarification I needed.

We continued to uncover details about my birth, with additional childhood memories surfacing and taking on new meaning.

When I was thirteen years old, my brother and I had been fooling around on the stairs. He was trying to go up and I was trying to go down. Neither of us was willing to move for the other, and consequently an argument broke out. As was typical between us as siblings, he threw out a nasty comment at me and I replied with an equally nasty comment. That banter went on for a bit until one of us started to wear down.

"Ha-ha!" he said that day, seemingly out of nowhere. "You're adopted!"

"Am not!"

"Yes you are!"

What happened next was so out of the ordinary, so out of left field, that it actually took the words out of both of our mouths. Our mother came around the corner from the kitchen where she had been listening in.

"Who told you that?" she demanded. She turned to look right at me. "Who told you that you were adopted?"

Due to her burning emotion, my brother and I looked at each other in absolute shock.

"Nobody," I said, raising both of my arms in surrender. "Nobody told me that. We were just being mean to each other. That's all!"

At that, I went downstairs and my brother headed upstairs.

When I reflected back on that conversation, I realized that my mother hadn't said anything to make it clear that I hadn't been adopted. In fact, from my recollection, she seemed more concerned with wanting to know who had told me.

❧

When I was in Grade Eleven, I was very excited to win a poetry contest at school.

"Your Aunt Victoria writes beautiful poetry too," my mother commented to me.

I took her statement for what it was, not knowing that Aunt Victoria was my biological mother. How amazing it is to think that we both, as mother and daughter, had been given that ability.

❧

At the luncheon following Victoria's funeral service, I was approached by Uncle George, one of Anne and Victoria's older brothers and my Aunt Isabel's husband. He was a calm and gentle spirit, easy to get along with. He was always very kind and loving towards me. I adored him and had deemed him in my heart as my favourite uncle.

After greeting me with a hug and a kiss, he said, "It must be very difficult for you to have just lost your mother and not being included with your brothers in the ceremony."

While standing there, I realized that even though I had grown to be much taller than he was, he was still a quiet giant in my life. I had fond memories of sitting on his lap when I was little, and I'd always felt safe and secure when I was with him. So when I heard him confuse Victoria with my mother, Anne, my heart sank.

Poor Uncle George, I thought. *He must have some dementia setting in. He doesn't remember who my mother is.*

"Oh, Uncle George," I said, lovingly yet sympathetically. "I'm sorry, you're confused. My mother was Anne. I'm one of Anne's kids!"

Uncle George simply nodded as he looked me in the eye.

"Okay," he said, shrugging his shoulders.

He turned and sat at the table behind us with his brother, my Uncle Phil. George slowly shook his downturned head, then released a deep sigh.

"She doesn't know!" he had said to his brother.

"Doesn't know what?" I had asked.

Uncle George and Uncle Phil glanced at each other with disbelieving looks on their faces. Then they spoke in what can only be described as some kind of double talk code, something only a brother would be able to understand.

Of course, I had no reason at that time to understand the depth of what my uncles had been discussing that day. But I was left quite puzzled by the conversation.

When my mother, Anne, passed away, my siblings and I stood as couples around the funeral home. I recalled watching my aunts and uncles as they went to my siblings to pay their respects, but they didn't come to Jake and me. At the time, I interpreted this non-acknowledgement to mean that there was something wrong with me. However, looking back, I realize that my aunts and uncles most likely assumed that I knew Anne wasn't my mother.

At one point in time, as I stood by my mother's casket, Uncle George came over to talk to me.

"So she was a good mother to you, was she?" he said.

At the time I thought it was a very unusual question, but I shook it off and gave him a simple answer.

ॐ

When I was sixteen years old, I was having supper with my mother and father. During our suppertime chatter, my father called me a "D.P.," to which my mother became very angry.

"Don't call her that!"

My father looked down at the table and concentrated on his food. My response was to come to my father's defence.

"What in the world!?" I said. "He was just calling me by my initials."

My father picked up on it and flatly added, "That's right! D.P."

As if it couldn't have meant anything else, I turned to my mother. "What did you think it meant?"

"It certainly doesn't stand for your initials," she curtly said. "D.P. stands for 'displaced person.' It was a term used during the war to refer to those people who couldn't go back to their families and were therefore sent somewhere else to live."

At that, my father and I kept quiet. I had no idea what she was talking about, nor did I understand her intended meaning. She didn't elaborate.

fifty-five

God Demonstrated His Love for Us

When I entered the living room, David smiled. His voice was tender and mellow, his intonation filled with care and concern.

"Hey! How are you?" he asked.

He lay on his side in a foetal position, disguising his height of six feet. His thin face and arms gave proof of a man whose body was dying. The head of his bed was slightly propped up and several pillows supported his frail torso.

My thoughts swirled with childhood memories. I remembered always being so excited when he had come over. I had loved him—his laughter, his tender heart, and of course his dimples. He was so cute! We'd always had so much fun together, playing outside, with the dog, in the old car graveyard next door. David and I had climbed into those old wrecks and pretended we were driving. However, as evidenced by him winning the Checker Flag in his teens, there was a chance he had pretended he was racing!

"So, how are you doing?" David asked, interrupting my thoughts.

"Me?" It seemed so bizarre to me that here he was, battling cancer, yet he had less regard for himself than he did for others. "I'm okay. Been a long day. I just wanted to drop in to see you for a bit before I went home."

Over the next several weeks, I dropped in on many occasions to check up on my little brother. During those visits, he and I laughed and giggled, and we grieved and lamented over the way our lives had been. Neither of us understood why Anne had kept me and sent him away, and we couldn't understand why our mother, Victoria, had fought for him yet given me up. It didn't make any sense to either of us.

Anger told me that I should resent Anne, that I should be livid with her that she had taken that position regarding David. After all, he had been a good kid. He had never gotten into trouble and never posed a problem for us. By that point in her life, some of her children were already grown and one had already left home. I couldn't understand why one more child would have made such a difference to her. At the same time, she had perhaps felt that she'd already done her part by taking me in.

Anger also told me that I should resent her for keeping me away from my biological mother. Even though Victoria had suffered from mental health concerns, that shouldn't have mattered; I should have known who she was. I strongly felt that a relationship with her should have been encouraged, even if it was minimal.

Anger seethed in me!

It wasn't joyful to share our childhood pains, but I knew with all sincerity that I could look him in the eye.

"I understand," I said, "But David, we can rejoice because we have each done the work to break the cycle of abuse. Let's praise God for that. What's more, it's not by chance that we have reconnected. God has brought us together and orchestrated all of this. Our opportunity to bond, talk, and share our love and our pains is not a mistake."

David just nodded. His already weak and frail hand trembled as he wiped tears away from his eyes.

"And how amazing, David!" I continued. "When we look back over our lives, we see that the Lord had been there with us through all of it. You and I, we were not alone. The Lord Jesus intervened in a mighty way in my life, and in yours! Especially when I recall how people came and walked beside me, supported me, and carried me through some very difficult times. Not only did He give us words of encouragement and strength, but He also gave us amazing spouses to support us. You have Doreen and I have Jake. God made no mistake when He brought them into our lives to love us unconditionally and to represent Christ's love to us through those very difficult seasons in our lives. God is so good, isn't He?"

My thoughts went back to the first time David and Doreen had come to our home after we'd found out that we were half-siblings. As he'd walked towards our house from his car, he had carried a planter that he and Doreen had purchased for our front porch. With his shoulders back and his head held high, I'd seen a peaceful look on his face, a look that had told me how happy he was to have found his sister and to have a place where he felt he belonged.

That evening, David, Doreen, Jake, and I had shared our life stories with each other and discovered that not only had each of us individually made a commitment to trust in Jesus Christ as our personal Saviour, but that we had also clearly recognized the grace of God that had carried us through such difficult times. The more we had talked and shared about the struggles we'd had as children, living with sadness, in poverty and dysfunction, the more apparent it had become that Jesus had been there with us the whole time. Not only had Jesus taken the penalty of our sin onto Himself when He died on the cross, but He'd also taken the burden of the sins committed against us. And in that we knew that Jesus understood our pain and hurt, because He had already bore the tears we shed.

Moreover, Jesus had the scars to prove His love for us.

But God demonstrates his own love for us in this: While we were still sinners, Christ died for us.

—Romans 5:8

fifty-six

Then It Was Time

April 2014

A COUPLE OF DAYS BEFORE HE PASSED AWAY, DAVID STARTED TO SEE the most extraordinary things. On one occasion, Doreen told me that David had stared at the ceiling in their living room. When Doreen had asked him what he was thinking about, he'd said, "Jesus," then explained that he was seeing Jesus's face on the ceiling in the stucco. Doreen had asked him to show her where.

"He's gone now," David had said. "But He'll be back."

On another occasion, David again pointed to the ceiling in their living room, but this time he was laughing. When Doreen asked him what he was laughing about, he said, "Moses. I see Moses!"

The next day, while Edward and Doreen were helping him readjust himself in his bed, David appeared startled and once again pointed to the ceiling.

"The light," he said, taking a deep breath. "The light is so beautiful!"

He had started to shake. With tears rolling down his cheeks, he'd lowered his head and become quiet, totally in awe of what he had experienced.

The Lord continued to open heaven up to David.

Then it was time.

I considered whether there might be an easy way to tell this part of the story, but there is none—no easy way to tell you that on April 3, 2014, David succumbed to the cancer that had plagued his body. Just three hundred and thirteen days after finding out that we were half-brother and sister, Doreen and her children, with Jake and me, watched as the Lord called David to heaven. His suffering was over and he entered glory.

We are confident, I say, and would prefer to be away from the body and at home with the Lord.
—2 Corinthians 5:8

As a child, when I had arrived home from school one day, David was gone. But the Lord reconnected us in an astounding yet humbling way. He gave us ten months to reunite as half-siblings and time to rebuild our relationship. He also gave us the opportunity to celebrate as full siblings through Christ, with the comfort and knowledge that we will be reunited again one day.

In my human weakness, it wasn't okay with me that David passed away and the hurt travelled into the deep chambers of my heart. But I was comforted in knowing that I would see David again and that we would have all of eternity together.

In the frailty of his infirmity, several hours before David died he looked at me and mouthed the words, "I love you."

"Love ya too," I simply replied. "See ya later!"

If I rise on the wings of the dawn, if I settle on the far side of the sea, even there your hand will guide me, your right hand will hold me fast. If I say, "Surely the darkness will hide me and the light become night around me," even the darkness will not be dark to you; the night will shine like the day, for darkness is as light to you.

—Psalm 139:9–12

fifty-seven

Darkness Returns

Darkness knocked and I let him in. He came disguised, lied, and called himself grief. Darkness led me to his place of despair, back to that place where hope was lost.

The anguish of losing my brother under those most unusual of circumstances was so deep, and the pain so tangible, that I knew I had to concentrate on something more positive in order to get me through the sorrow. So I focused on the upcoming birth of our sixth grandchild. I anticipated my joy and excitement upon hearing whether it was a boy or a girl and what his or her name would be.

Then, out of nowhere, came a seemingly audible thought: "I bet nobody was excited when you were born!"

I immediately crumbled under the weight of the accumulated rubble of my life.

It's true, I thought, breaking down in a torrent of tears. *It's all true!*

The realization hit home that I had been the product of a family scandal that was kept secret for nearly six decades. I had found my brother only to lose him again after such a short period of time. I had been lied to; I felt cheated. My former feelings of being unwanted and useless returned as I was carried into a gutter of wretchedness.

As I attempted to make sense of this groundswell of emotion, more thoughts crowded my mind: *I was just a scandal! My mother gave me away! No one wanted me! Nobody loves me! Everyone hates me! Instead of being a precious wee babe, I was a problem!*

When I had found out that Victoria was my mother, I'd deferred my feelings in order to place my emotional energies on David.

I knew that I had no control over what had happened to me, but my negative thoughts and feelings about myself threw me back into that dark place where I felt awful about myself, angry, hopelessly lost, and in a downcast spirit of gloom. I wanted to find a place to hide. That was all that depression needed to move right back in.

I fell headfirst into a deep hole, with anger and fear lurking in the darkness.

Anger found dark corners to hide in my mind, stirring up petty annoyances within me which caused resentment and bitterness. Anger taunted me in my bewilderment and gave me reasons to be infuriated and full of rage. Anger bombarded me with the injustice of the entire situation. Anger reminded me that no one had cared enough about me to have told me the truth. Anger reminded me of my father's philandering behaviours and the shame I carried because of that. Although I knew Victoria hadn't had the capacity to raise me, I was infuriated to think that inasmuch as my aunts had been worried someone might get hurt when the truth was exposed, in the end it was me who had gotten hurt.

I was forced to face the truth of my emotions and of the entire situation.

I didn't want Victoria to be my mother! She was the aunt who had scared me and made me feel uncomfortable when she stared at me. I questioned my ability to be compassionate and loving.

What kind of person am I? I asked myself.

I was ashamed of my father and embarrassed to be connected to him in any way. I was angry because he hadn't shared the truth with me about the identity of my mother and had allowed me to live in the untruths. My spirit cried out, *What was he thinking?* I felt that my life had been lived as a lie. How many times had people laughed at me behind my back?

When my second child had been born, I had commented about how much she looked like Aunt Victoria. One might think that would have been a perfect opportunity for someone to have told me the truth.

When I thought of special events in my life, like my wedding to Jake, I wanted to scream. I realized that my father's desire for Jake and me to elope had been in order to avoid a potential conflict at the wedding with Victoria. He may also have been nervous that in planning the wedding I would find out the truth about her being my biological mother. It also saddened me that my own mother, Victoria, hadn't even been there; she and her new husband had chosen not to attend. I recognized that it would have been painful for her to attend, but anger proudly raised its ugly head and bitterly reminded me that *someone* should have told me. I should have had the opportunity to get to know my own flesh and blood.

Anger raged in me like a thunderous storm which could not be calmed. I could not be pacified.

What do I do with all of this anger? I thought. *Where do I go to still the rage inside me?*

I wanted to throw things, to hit someone as a means to expel my anger. But I knew that it would be wrong to lash out at those I loved, at those I truly admired. My soul cried out and I attempted to find a way to vent, to find a healthy way to express the exasperation, but I dreaded doing the wrong thing. Instead I listened to fear's sneering voice: "Turn it inward, turn it inward. There is no safe place to go. There is no safe place to hide. Hold onto anger. Hide him deep inside."

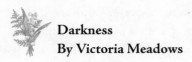

Darkness
By Victoria Meadows

Darkness
Such a shadowy feeling lies
Here and there
Except the skies
And little stars peep through
The velvet darkness of the night
Where all is invisible
'Til darkness turns to light

fifty-eight

From Darkness to Light

I FELT HOPELESSLY LOST, DOOMED IN A WORLD OF EXISTING FROM moment to moment, day to day. I was in a spirit of gloom, imprisoned in dungeons in my mind where there was no light. No light meant that there were no shadows. Sightless, I grappled for security, sanctuary, and a sense of belonging. There seemed to be no way for me to be redirected back to the surface.

I had once read, concerning Spurgeon,

What he suffered in these times of darkness we may not know. They usually accompanied his days and nights of physical agony under the strength of a gout attack, and even his desperate calling upon God often brought him no relief. "There are dungeons," he said, "beneath the Castle of Despair," and he had often been in them.[7]

Somehow I felt that I could identify with him.

For many years I had been haunted by the illusion of a little girl. I knew that it wasn't a real little girl; in my heart I knew that it was an evil spirit, although I never felt a sense of evil when she appeared. This presence would appear in the form of a child-sized silhouette. I called her my little girl because she seemed so innocent and calm. I sometimes talked to

---

7   Arnold A. Dallimore, *C.H. Spurgeon: The New Biography* (Chicago, IL: Moody Press, 1984), 186.

her when she showed up and said things to her like "So there you are!" or "I haven't seen you in a while."

I realized after a time that the spirit presented herself to me when I was under incredible stress at work.

My pastor warned me, "Do not talk to the spirit!"

I didn't always heed that warning, because when darkness loomed over me, I felt such a sense of evil that fear attempted to control me. When I was in that dark place, the illusion was more intense and appeared more often.

That dark place in my mind led me to believe that perhaps I was truly crazy.

But when I found out that Victoria was my biological mother, I started to question whether perhaps she might have been misdiagnosed; after all, she had also believed in Jesus Christ as her Saviour. Was it possible that what she dealt with wasn't paranoid schizophrenia at all, but something spiritual? Conversely, I had always assumed that what I had struggled with had been spiritual, but then I started to wonder whether my struggle was psychological. Although I knew better, I did question whether it was possible that I had paranoid schizophrenia.

Those disturbing thoughts added burden to my load as I cried out for freedom from spiritual oppression. Since David's death, I had buried all my pain and tried to live a normal life. I had pretended that it was all a dream because I knew that if I looked at that pain directly in the face, I would have to admit the truth and the reality of everything that had happened. So, in an effort to ease my emotional load, I talked to myself on my commute to and from work, trying to sort out the negative thoughts and feelings.

Many years earlier, I had shared my struggles of sexual abuse, depression, and suicidal ideation with my pastor and his wife. Those were difficult yet necessary discussions and it was definitely hard work to change my way of thinking. I again reached out to my pastor and his wife, and laid all my heartache and confusion before them.

After I spent several minutes lamenting my life and my woes regarding the identity of my biological mother, I also described to them the things I had pieced together about Victoria's life—what I knew, what I remembered as a child, and what David had told me about her. I also shared my dilemma of wondering whether my struggle wasn't spiritual but psychological. I knew that I didn't have paranoid schizophrenia, but I was so downcast in my spirit that I honestly felt like I was losing it.

Finally, I asked them, "Do you think I'm crazy?"

Almost simultaneously, they both replied, "Absolutely not!"

I told them about the emotional pain that had surfaced in me since David had died. I then heard myself declare out loud exactly what my thoughts were about myself.

"Nobody celebrated when I was born," I said. "I was a problem from the moment Victoria found out she was pregnant with me."

"Whose child are you, Darlene?" my pastor asked, challenging me.

"I don't even know anymore."

"You do know." He paused before continuing. "You are Christ's child!"

I knew that. I knew that I belonged to Jesus and that my identity was in Him and no other. I knew that Jesus loved me. It was what I had taught my children to believe about themselves. I knew enough Scripture to know that God knows all about me and that He made me.

For you created my inmost being; you knit me together in my mother's womb.

—Psalm 139:13

I knew that I couldn't choose who my mother and father were, but I could choose to have Jesus as my Heavenly Father. I knew that I was a child of God.

I knew all this—in my head. But at that moment, I realized that I didn't really know it in my heart. In many ways, I had not claimed it as my own. I had believed the truth for my children, that Jesus loved them, but I hadn't claimed it for me. Perhaps I had believed it once, when I was a child, but somehow I had lost it as an adult. After going through so much, it seemed impossible for me to come to any kind of logical reasoning or real acceptance of His love for me.

For many years, my world felt fractured. Knowing the truth regarding the identity of my biological mother and then losing David blew my world apart.

I am a child of God, I thought. At first it was a captivating thought. Then I fought against it and argued with God that it didn't apply to me. However, as hard as I fought against this truth, I kept hearing it repeated over and over in my mind.

I am a child of God.

So I reached out and grabbed on to this truth. I held it tightly. It was the start of a journey that moved me out of a wandering state of confusion, out of the depths of despair, towards a place where I eventually felt a sense of belonging and love.

I am a child of God.

I asked myself whether I sincerely believed in Jesus and the message of the cross. I also asked myself whether I believed that He had presented me with His amazing grace and then lavished His love on me, whether I believed that He had sent His Son, Jesus Christ, to love me, die for me, save me, and bridge the gap between my sinfulness and God the Father. I asked myself whether I believed that He walked with me hand in hand.

If I believed those things, then I had no other option but to conclude that I was (and am) His child.

"Darlene," I heard him say. "You are my child!"

Yet to all who did receive him, to those who believed in his name, he gave the right to become children of God—children born not of natural descent, nor of human decision or a husband's will, but born of God.

—John 1:12–13

Born of God.

Born of God!

A sense of calm suddenly came over me. It was an unexplainable perfect peace that surpassed all understanding.

And the peace of God, which transcends all understanding, will guard your hearts and your minds in Christ Jesus.

—Philippians 4:7

I basked in His presence and, like an infant child, began to simply rest in His loving arms. I recognized that He had moulded and shaped me into a new creature, a new individual.

Therefore, if anyone is in Christ, the new creation has come; the old has gone, the new is here!

—2 Corinthians 5:17

❧

I don't know the details of how I ended up with Louis and Anne, but I do know, according to my sister Annette, that one day, when she arrived home from school, there was a new baby in the house: a baby girl with dark hair and long eyelashes. According to Annette, Anne and Louis had been having a discussion about what the baby's name should be. Louis had wanted to call me Darlene Phyllis and Anne had wanted to call me Phyllis Darlene. As they couldn't come to a decision, they asked Annette to break the tie. Since Annette liked the name Darlene Phyllis, that became my name.

Many years later, David asked me what my middle name was. When I told him that it was Phyllis, he shared with me that Victoria's favourite girl's name was Phyllis. Later, David and I read some of our mother's poetry and discovered so many poems that referred to "Darling." David believed that these had been written about me.

I had always understood my name to mean "darling" or "loved one," and I always understood my middle name to mean "to love." Together, therefore, my name meant "loved one to love."

When I finally understood that I was God's child, it blew me away to think that God had already given me the right name. When I reflected on my name, and claimed it for its true meaning, it became a significant commemoration of not only my new understanding of myself but a clear understanding of my true identity in Christ.

I could hear Christ speaking to me: "You are mine, my precious darling daughter, loved one to love."

Do not fear, for I have redeemed you; I have summoned you by name; you are mine.

—Isaiah 43:1

Your eyes saw my unformed body; all the days ordained for me were written in your book before one of them came to be. How precious to me are your thoughts, God! How vast is the sum of them! Were I to count them, they would outnumber the grains of sand—when I awake, I am still with you.

—Psalm 139:16–18

Secure

Nothing can separate me from the love of God
For in His Holy Spirit I am sealed
Surely when all darkness surrounds me by day
His endless love for me is revealed

Within the masterful works of His skillful hands
He paints my world in a mood of joy
Entreating me to sing praises to Him
While in my heart His love employs

Within the hearts of men He sets His spirit aflame
Equipping them to show me His love
He promises everlasting hope when all else fails
And a strength that comes from above

He floods my life as He pours into my heart
His awesome love so abundantly
Keeping me secure in His almighty Being
No. Nothing can separate Him from me.

fifty-nine

> *"For my thoughts are not your thoughts, neither are your ways
> my ways," declares the Lord. "As the heavens are higher than the
> earth, so are my ways higher than your ways and my thoughts
> than your thoughts."*
>
> —Isaiah 55:8–9

ALTHOUGH I KNEW I COULDN'T THINK LIKE GOD, I WONDERED
whether I should try to think about myself the way God thinks about me.
In order to do that, I needed to believe that I was God's child. I needed to
claim God's love for me and replace the lies I had believed about myself
with biblical statements about what God believed about me.

It therefore became necessary to change my thoughts from "Nobody
loves me; everybody hates me" to "Our Heavenly Father loves me; He
cannot and does not hate something He created." Once my belief system
started to change, I developed statements that I then repeated to myself in
order to counteract the lies: "I am God's child," "The Lord Jesus loves me,"
"He found me so valuable that He died for me," "The Holy Spirit loves me
and sent people into my life who love and care for me," and "My family
loves me and honours me as their wife, mother, caregiver, sister, sister-in-
law, and friend."

God couldn't help Himself. He loved me because it was the essence
and nature of His character. In fact, *"God is love"* (1 John 4:16). Furthermore, His love for me is so great that He has lavished it on me.

See what great love the Father has lavished on us, that we should be
called children of God! And that is what we are!

—1 John 3:1

That is what I am: God's child.

Because He is love and because I am His child, He gives me an abundance of love, so much that I cannot even begin to understand the enormity of this truth. So when God said that He lavished His love on me, I needed to realize that it was already the best, most wonderful, and most abundant love that could ever exist.

Ultimately, He showed His love to me in such a magnificent way by sacrificing Himself so that I could live with Him forever.

This is how God showed his love among us: He sent his one and
only Son into the world that we might live through him. This is love:
not that we loved God, but that he loved us and sent his Son as an
atoning sacrifice for our sins.

—1 John 4:9–10

Nothing is too hard for God. Nothing can separate me from the love of God. Nothing can be done to me that will change His love for me. I can do nothing to earn salvation, and I can do nothing to earn His love. He did it all!

Because of these revelations in my thinking, I finally rested and snuggled safe in His arms of love—no matter what. All the emotional pain and baggage that was tied to that emotional pain was part of my life's story. But in spite of all that, I was able to lay it down because I knew He loved me that much.

God is love!

I am a child of God.

☙

Over the years, on many occasions, I have asked Jake, "Do you love me?"
His reply is consistently the same. "Yup!"

So I would then seek more details. "Why do you love me?"

"Because. Just because."

One day, he documented some of his reasons in a love letter to me. In part of that letter, he wrote, "Darlene: You are worthy of my love BE-CAUSE!! YOU!!"

It amazed me to think that Jake told me I was worthy of his love simply because of who I was and not because of anything I had done, would do, or even could do. It was such a simple expression of the meaning of unconditional love.

It made me wonder, *If my husband has the ability to love me unconditionally, then how much more does God love me?*

Still uncertain of that love, one day while sitting quietly I wrestled with the Lord, lamenting over my life and the things that had happened.

"Lord, do you love me?" I asked Him. I continued before he had a chance to answer. "And then, Lord, if you love me, why?"

That was when I heard the Lord's still small voice. "It is not a matter of whether I love you, but because I love you!"

Still struggling, I replied, "Then why, Lord? Why do you love me?"

His answer blew me away! "You see, Darlene, My love for you isn't based on anything you have done or could ever do. Rather it is based on who I *am*. I died for you because I *am* love. That should be sufficient reason to say that you are worthy of My love."

Such a beautiful twist! I needed to only believe He had found me worthy of His love because of who He is.

Certainly Jesus doesn't need my love, nor does He need my praise. Rather, He wants my love, He wants a relationship with me, and He wants my adoration. After all, I am His child. I am His daughter. Thus, I am called to love Him with all of my being.

> *Love the Lord your God with all your heart and with all your soul and with all your strength and with all your mind.*
>
> —Luke 10:27

I haven't totally grasped the magnitude and depth of the love God has for me and for others. But as I've grown in understanding the depth of the love Jesus has for me, I have grown closer to Him and gained a deeper insight into my relationship with Him. Indeed, the reverse is also true: as I have grown closer to Him and gained a deeper insight into my relationship with Him, my understanding of the depth of His love for me has also grown.

> *I love you, Lord, my strength. The Lord is my rock, my fortress and my deliverer; my God is my rock, in whom I take refuge, my shield and the horn of my salvation, my stronghold. I called to the Lord, who is worthy of praise, and I have been saved from my enemies.*
> —Psalm 18:1–3

God goes the extra mile over and over again. Despite who I was and despite my human frailty, God still says that I was created for His glory!

> *Bring my sons from afar and my daughters from the ends of the earth—everyone who is called by my name, whom I created for my glory, whom I formed and made.*
> —Isaiah 43:6–7

Who does that?
God does.

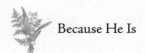 Because He Is

Undeserving love is what He gave to me
When Jesus chose to die at Calvary
Cherishing me as one who is worthy
To be loved, simply because He is

Compassionately He reaches His hand in mine
And draws me close to His side. Love divine
Carrying me in His arms. Shielding me
Near His breast. And simply because He is

Nevertheless there's nothing I can do to earn
Christ's favour. Except to try to learn
That forgiveness is His gracious gift
To me. He loves me simply because He is.

sixty

*Now Israel loved Joseph more than any of his other sons, because he
had been born to him in his old age; and he made an ornate robe for
him. When his brothers saw that their father loved him more than
any of them, they hated him and could not speak a kind word to him.*
—Genesis 37:3–4

I HELD MY HUSBAND'S HAND AS WE WALKED DOWN THE LANEWAY
together. I loved being with him and felt so proud to be his wife. While we
walked, I chattered and he listened as I told him how much I had always
loved and appreciated the Bible story of Joseph.

Joseph had known his brothers hated him because their father loved
him more than them, and because he had interpreted his own dream to
mean that he would one day rule over them and their father. Unfortunately, Joseph's brothers turned against him, plotted to kill him, and sub-
sequently sold him as a slave to a caravan of Ishmaelite wanderers. I often
wondered whether that act of betrayal made Joseph question whether he
had misinterpreted his own dreams. After all, becoming a slave was fairly
good evidence that his brothers weren't going to bow down to him.

Miraculously, Joseph ended up in Potiphar's court, where many people served him and trusted him. Unfortunately, Potiphar's wife lied about
Joseph and he ended up in prison. Joseph was punished for doing the
right thing. There appeared to be no justice for her vengeful act.

Amazingly, the Scriptures record that even after all the adversities he
had gone through, Joseph still trusted God, because he believed that *"the*

Lord was with him; he showed him kindness and granted him favor in the eyes of the prison warden" (Genesis 39:21).

As only God can, details of Joseph's life were orchestrated in order to eventually free him and elevate him to a place of importance. It wasn't a mistake that the cupbearer and baker were imprisoned at the same time as Joseph. Joseph interpreted their dreams, reassuring the cupbearer that he would return to Pharaoh's court and telling the baker that he would lose his life. The cupbearer promised Joseph that he would speak to Pharaoh on Joseph's behalf when he was released from prison. However, two years passed before he remembered his promise. When Pharaoh had dreams of his own, the cupbearer told him about Joseph's ability to interpret dreams. Joseph was then brought before Pharaoh, Joseph interpreted Pharaoh's dreams, and Joseph was once again elevated to a position of authority in order to prepare for Egypt's coming years of famine.

In spite of all that Joseph had gone through, he acknowledged his pain and was still grateful to God.

Joseph named his firstborn Manasseh and said, "It is because God has made me forget all my trouble and all my father's household." The second son he named Ephraim and said, "It is because God has made me fruitful in the land of my suffering."
—Genesis 41:51–52

God had Joseph do all of the heart work even before his brothers were brought back into his life. Then, since Joseph had forgiven his brothers before he saw them, he was able to say to them, *"You intended to harm me, but God intended it for good to accomplish what is now being done, the saving of many lives"* (Genesis 50:20).

Through all of Joseph's hardships and trials, even though he didn't know the end of his story or the results that would come from his obedience to God, he still believed in God's greater purpose. Joseph saying God meant it for good doesn't mean that God's hand was in the evil; rather, Joseph simply meant that God used the evil and turned it to good. That's one of God's strategies: to turn evil things to good.

As a result of this train of thought, I realized that I had often missed the purpose of the wounds in my life.

Jake quietly listened as I shared. At times he held my hand and at other times I waved my hands, expressing emotions and emphasizing words as I spoke. He listened and acknowledged my train of thought, which eventually took me to my final point.

"I get that Joseph was mistreated and that he had ups and downs in his life, and I get that God used him and then turned the atrocious events in Joseph's life into something good," I said. "I get all of that. But what I don't get is how all of this that has happened to me can have any meaning in my life, because quite frankly I don't see that any good has come from all that I have been through."

Without skipping a beat, Jake quickly reflected on what I had said. "Are you kidding me? Have you taken a look at my life? Because of what you've been through, I have become a changed man: God has strengthened my faith. You see, God has used these horrible things which harmed you in order to change me for the good."

I felt so humbled by his reply and loved him for his insight. It became so apparent to me that *"in all things God works for the good of those who love him, who have been called according to his purpose"* (Romans 8:28). My point here is simply to bring attention to God and His sovereignty, because I finally realized that things didn't come into my life without first going through His loving hands. I finally understood that He had allowed those things in my life in order to bring me closer to Him.

When Joseph's brothers, Potiphar's wife, and the cupbearer inflicted wounds on him, Joseph had to keep his eyes on God and trust in Him because only God knew the rest of the story. Rather than focusing on the explanations he needed for his pain, Joseph lived in the faith of trusting God, not knowing what would happen next. I learned from Joseph that I needed to be fully conscious of the fact that I was asking God to explain the reasons for my pain rather than trusting Him to carry me through it.

That became one more step towards the healing I was seeking towards both my mental and spiritual health.

෨

Two months following David's death, on a Sunday morning, I heard a pastor make this statement: "God has given you a story. Now respond to it." Although I was aware that the pastor was preaching to hundreds of people, it felt like God was speaking directly to me.

Prior to hearing this, I had heard the Lord tell me in many different ways on many different occasions that He wanted me to tell my story.

"So what?" I replied every time the Lord gave me this direction. "I have this huge, messed-up life! It's not like anyone cares or wants to hear about my story. So what!?"

I was blowing Him off. God had given me a job to do, and rather than be compliant I turned my head in another direction and invited anger to come and sit right down beside me.

Then I heard anger whisper bitterness and resentment in my ear: "Why should you have to share your story? You don't even like many parts of your life. Won't it just renew the pain you've had to deal with? It's not fair!"

So when God commanded me to share my story, I responded with annoyance and anger.

"Why?" I asked Him. "Why should I talk about it?"

"Because the story of your life, Darlene, isn't about you! It's about Me." I was humbled.

I knew that God had written my story.

...all the days ordained for me were written in your book before one of them came to be.

—Psalm 139:16

I imagined God as He sat and thought about me, as He designed, moulded, and shaped me. I envisioned God sitting on His throne, writing my story while the angels sang glories in the background. He didn't scribble it down without any planning or forethought. Rather, He lovingly and carefully penned every detail, orchestrating all aspects to bring about His perfect plan for me.

I imagined the leaves of the pages of the book open on His desk. I could see the lines of text as He inscribed the words of my life. Giving allowance for me to make decisions and choices and mistakes—lots of them—he left some pages blank. But what really moved me was when I saw the places where He had interlineated special edit notes, written in red ink. Notes that went something like this:

+   Especially support Darlene here.
+   Make a lily of the valley plant grow here.
+   Add a moment of joy here.
+   Hugs are perfect at this time.
+   Uplift her through music there.
+   Show her that You can be trusted.
+   Reveal Yourself to her through prayer here.
+   Tap Jake on the shoulder to remind her that he loves her.
+   Carry Darlene here.
+   Bless her with a child to love. Make it three! Grandchildren as a bonus!
+   Shelter her in the shadow of your wings.
+   Teach her about grace and hope.
+   Tell Hildi to call her here.
+   Allow her to fail here.
+   Help her to forgive others as she learns about My forgiveness for her.
+   Pain and grief are part of her life here.
+   Love her, just love her.
+   Spirit, nudge others to pray for her here.

As only one of over seven billion people on the planet, God took the time to think about me, plan for me, and write about me. How magnificent it is to think that He does this for each and every one of His children. What would I do without Jesus?

If only you, God, would slay the wicked! Away from me, you who are bloodthirsty! They speak of you with evil intent; your adversaries misuse your name. Do I not hate those who hate you, Lord, and abhor those who are in rebellion against you? I have nothing but hatred for them; I count them my enemies.

—Psalm 139:19–22

sixty-one

Paradox

When I was a teen, one of my hideaways was Dieppe Park, located in downtown Windsor on the shore of the Detroit River. I sat quietly on an old park bench as I took in the Detroit skyline and watched the passersby. I was in a public place and therefore not alone, but I was alone in my thoughts as I ruminated about the problems I had at home.

I tried to talk to God and asked Him to help me understand why He would allow such pain on earth, particularly as it related to the way people treated each other. I pleaded with Him to reveal Himself to me. I asked Him to help me, and to help me in my part of the world where I felt so much hurt. I asked Him to give me hope because I felt like things were so hopeless.

It was many years later when I learned about my father and his phi-landering escapades. While I was at home alone one evening, my sister Clara called me.

"I have something to tell you," she said.

She proceeded to tell me about my father's affair in the 1950s when he had abandoned his family and left for the United States, only to be found, charged, and returned to Canada. We didn't know the name of the woman he had left with, we didn't know what had happened to their child, and we were unaware of my father's additional affair with Aunt Victoria.

When I later discovered information in the newspaper that outlined details of my father's exploits, I realized that as a teen I had been sitting very close to the exact spot where my father had strewn his personal be-longings along the riverfront. I was humbled at God's amazing hand in my life. I recognized that I had been seeking peace for my family and in my life at the same place where a wicked plan had been played out to bring us so much pain and turmoil.

Hatred for my father burned inside me. I was tired of what that man had done. All of it. As I worked through the truth about my birth, my life, and the lies, I became all too aware of the fact that I wanted my father to be punished. When I reflected on all his crimes and wrongdoings, though, I realized how much it still impacted me and my offspring. I resented him and the legacy he had left for me.

In the middle of my fury towards my father, I came face to face with myself and my sin: my disobedience to God, my rebellion, my hatred, my anger, and my unforgiving spirit. I then recalled that many years earlier I had prayed to forgive my father for the things he had done to me. Afterwards, feelings of revenge had returned, at which time I vacillated between forgiveness and contempt. I then learned that in order to make the forgiveness stick, I needed to forgive over and over again.

Once again I was faced with having to make a choice—a choice between living in the bitterness of unforgiveness or in the freedom of forgiveness. In addition, I had to find a resolution for what seemed to be a contradiction in my belief system: that even though God is love, He hates sin.

It was in that paradox that I had to once again release my need to punish my father and allow God to have His rightful place, to allow God to judge my father's heart.

Search me, God, and know my heart; test me and know my anxious thoughts. See if there is any offensive way in me, and lead me in the way everlasting.

—Psalm 139:23–24

sixty-two

Restoration

THE RESTORATION IN MY LIFE CAME SLOWLY. MY EMOTIONAL SCARS reminded me of the hurt and pain in my life, but those same scars also reminded me of the healing I had experienced.

I remember my affliction and my wandering, the bitterness and the gall. I well remember them, and my soul is downcast within me. Yet this I call to mind and therefore I have hope: because of the Lord's great love we are not consumed, for his compassions never fail. They are new every morning; great is your faithfulness.
—Lamentations 3:19–23

Many years earlier, when I realized that I needed additional help working through the effects of the sexual abuse, I had attended a support group. The facilitator had promised those who were there that God would return to us twofold. I remember thinking that I would be happy if God would just not let me completely lose my mind! I then discovered a verse in the book of Joel and claimed it as His promise to me that one day He would restore me and my life.

As time went on and I moved towards healing, I became aware that God had returned to me a thousand fold. He had blessed me with the best husband, a husband who went to the ends of the earth for me, supported me, cherished me, cared about me, prayed for me, and represented Christ's unconditional love. In addition, I had been blessed with three beautiful and precious daughters, two sons-in-law, and six most amazing grandchildren.

Twenty-two years following those first horrifying memories, and only eighteen months after my brother David's death, I spent a weekend laughing, eating, talking, and celebrating my sixtieth birthday. I was surrounded by the love of my husband and family. When all the festivities were over and everyone had headed home, I climbed into bed exhausted but extremely happy. As I laid my head on my pillow, Joel 2:25 resounded in my spirit: *"I will repay you for the years the locusts have eaten."*

 Sheltered

A new darkness draped over me
Enveloped me
and
Surrounded me

Today the darkness lifted
And with it came a gentle push
To move ahead

I stepped out
Then with all curiosity
I turned, longing to discover
Needing to understand
What this new darkness had been

Blinded by the holiness of His presence
I was humbled
My head looked down. I saw it there.
Laying before me on the ground
Was His image
Reflected in a shadowy shape
Feathering its way in softness
Entreating me to come closer
Gently enfolding me
Enveloping me
Surrounding me
Wrapping me in darkness
While drawing me close to the light
Close to His breast

And then I understood
I was in the shelter of His wings

Postscript

He will cover you with his feathers, and under his wings you will find refuge.

—Psalm 91:4

I no longer needed to hide in dark places like under the porch, in the attic, or in the dark corners of my mind, because I had discovered that my refuge was beneath His feathers, near the beat of His heart. I learned that I could run to Jesus at any time because He listened and answered my prayers.

In the morning, Lord, you hear my voice; in the morning I lay my requests before you and wait expectantly.

—Psalm 5:3

One day, I admired my friend Hildi's garden. Although she was an avid gardener, I asked why she had planted her lilies of the valley in the full sun. From my childhood experience, lilies of the valley had always grown in dark places.

Hildi's eyes grew wide. "Oh no, Darlene! Lilies of the valley actually thrive in the full bright sun!"

My heart flooded with a surge of warmth and love at the realization that God had specifically placed my lily of the valley under the front porch with me—just for me!

At times I had been so afraid of darkness and his angels that I'd believed the lies of Satan. I'd gone down paths that were destructive and detrimental for both my spiritual and physical well-being. But as my pastor used to say, I learned that dungeon experiences can be a blessing, because they help us to appreciate the light. The truth is that God is light and there is no darkness in Him at all.

Although I knew that Jesus Christ had died for my sins, I had made the discovery that Jesus Christ actually conquered sin and Satan. I finally understood that darkness will not overcome me.

I have struggled to understand why He saved me from self-harm while others fell deeper into the depths of despair, because I know that He loved them as well. I therefore acknowledged Him as sovereign and admitted that He always knows best. That was when I stopped arguing with God and acquiesced to living without knowing the answer to all the why questions.

God consistently used His written word to minister to me and encourage me. It was through His word that He spoke to me, and that is where I found healing.

He sent out His word and healed them.

—Psalm 107:20

...I am the Lord, who heals you.

—Exodus 15:26

He heals the brokenhearted and binds up their wounds.

—Psalm 147:3

...and by His wounds we are healed.

—Isaiah 53:5

Jesus lay down His life for me on the cross, and there He won victory over evil. At the cross, He gave me new life, a Saviour, a Father, a relationship with Him, and healing. At the cross, all things in my life were turned to God, and turned to good. At the cross, He forgave me and wants me to forgive others.

> *Be kind and compassionate to one another, forgiving each other,*
> *just as in Christ God forgave you.*
> —Ephesians 4:32

I discovered friction between the words "forgive" and "forget," and I realized that it's all right to forgive and remember because real forgiveness doesn't mean that you forget what happened. In fact, I likely will never forget about it because of the importance of these events in my life. In addition, by remembering how God has turned my life into something so beautiful, I am able to humbly thank Him and praise Him.

The Lord challenged me not to dwell on the past and to forget the things of the past long enough to see today and the possibility for tomorrow, because there is so much more yet to come.

> *Forget the former things; do not dwell on the past. See, I am doing*
> *a new thing! Now it springs up; do you not perceive it?*
> —Isaiah 43:18–19

Since God has carried me through the troubles of the past, I know that He will also carry me through the new things that will spring up for me.

It was a humbling exercise to have asked the Lord to search me. "Lord," I said. "Here I am and here is my heart. Take a look and talk to me. How am I doing?"

After all that I've been through, you might be asking, "How are you doing now?" Well, I'm aware that new things will spring up for me and that this may include hardships, struggles, and pain. But I'm confident that my hope is in my Heavenly Father, my Daddy who will always hold my hand and walk with me through those difficulties. I also hope that I will always believe in His love for me.

I still have my ups and downs, and at times I still struggle with the ongoing negative thoughts and feelings that come into my mind. I am fully aware that anger, darkness, fear, and despair are part of me and part

284 • Amazing Grace, Abounding Love

of my thoughts, not separate entities as personified in this story. But there are times when it feels like I'm in a persistent battle to not fall prey to them and keep my mind focused on being God's child, His daughter, and to always remember that He loves me!

On other days, it's easy to remain focused on hope.

There are times when I battle feelings of jealousy, especially when I hear people talk about their moms and dads. Father's Day and Mother's Day both bring me incredible sadness. At those times, I feel cheated, but then I flip the coin and see the blessings I have been given as a wife, mother, sister, and sister-in-law.

I deeply grieve that I didn't know my biological mother and still grieve the loss of the mother who raised me. Although we certainly had our difficulties, I'm thankful to her for taking me in and loving me as if I was her own. I now understand her comment: "You can't save them all, Darlene!" She had been speaking about herself that day. When I consider what my life might have been like if I had stayed with my biological mother, I am grateful that my Aunt Anne saved one.

I also deeply grieve the loss of my brother, David. I rejoice that we found each other and I'm grateful for the time we did have together, but I do miss him. Deeply.

I now feel that I belong. I can walk with my head up because I am a child of God and know that my place in Him has absolutely nothing to do with who my parents were. God has no grandchildren, only children, and I am His darling daughter. I belong to Him!

Truly, this is not yet the end of the story, my story, God's story. My hope is that as you have seen the hand of God at work in my life, you have also seen Him as the main character of this story.

My hope is that despite the things that have happened to you, you too will believe that Jesus's death on the cross and His resurrection from the grave is His amazing gift of grace and forgiveness for you—because of who He is and because of His abounding love for you.

As you live out your story, may you see it as God's story, and may you wholeheartedly be able to say, "I am a child of God!"

About the Author

Darlene Martens and her husband Jake have been married for more than forty years and continue to live in southern Ontario.

She is a graduate from the University of Windsor with a Master of Social Work. In addition, she holds a Bachelor of Social Work from the University of Manitoba and a Bachelor of Arts in Social Development Studies from the University of Waterloo. She is registered with the Ontario College of Social Workers and Social Services Workers (OCSWS-SW) and the Ontario Association of Social Workers (OASW).

Darlene works as a clinical social worker/therapist and has helped hurting people find healing.

She has served in a variety of roles in the church, including teaching Sunday school and serving as a deacon. She has also been commissioned as a Stephen Minister. Her passion is to see others put their faith in Jesus Christ as their Saviour and to rest safe and secure in His loving arms, knowing that they are children of God.

You can connect with Darlene at:
darlenemartensauthor.com